THE IDEAL CHRISTIAN HOME

The Ideal Christian Home

With Its

Sacred Sphere and Extensive Mission

By

J. S. SHOEMAKER

Give ear, O my people, to my law: incline your ears to the words of my mouth.

That the generation to come might know them, even the children which should be born, who should arise and declare them to their children:

That they might set their hope in God, and not forget the works of God, but keep his commandments.—Psa. 78:1, 6, 7.

Published by

MENNONITE PUBLISHING HOUSE

SCOTTDALE,   PENNSYLVANIA

1925

TO OUR DEAR CHILDREN,
  The souls which were divinely given to us;

TO ALL OUR POSTERITY,
  In whose best welfare we are greatly interested;

TO OUR BELOVED CHURCH
  And its forthcoming generations,

THIS VOLUME IS AFFECTIONATELY DEDICATED

THE IDEAL CHRISTIAN HOME

Expressions of Commendation on the New Book Entitled

I desire to say that I think it very good.—J. H. Mosemann.

This coming work I consider a most valuable contribution to our literature. It will be a book that is deserving of wide circulation within and without the Church. This book is designed to deal with the inner fabric of the Home and appeals to society in general, in a way that is most timely for meeting many vital issues that loom up in one of the critical situations of our time.

May the Lord bless this coming book to the end intended and may thousands of readers be made better husbands, wives and children by its perusal.—L. J. Heatwole.

I have just gone over your manuscript which, in my judgment, promises to be one of the most useful and practical books for the home that I have ever read, especially for our own people, in which is included, beside all the good material you get in other books of this nature the special points peculiar to our own Church. "Well done" my faithful brother.—D. H. Bender.

Your book on "The Ideal Home" has been read with great interest. I think that you have chosen a subject that needed to be presented to our people. I praise the Lord that He moved you to write as you did, that you say what you do, especially in the chapters dealing with husband and wife's relationship. Many writers forget that here is the place where homes are made or ruined.

Wishing you everything well in this work that you have undertaken for the Lord.—Oscar Burkholder.

I have read the manuscript for your proposed book "The Ideal Home," and in my judgment it is well written and should find a place in many a library. May God bless you and the work you have done in getting out this book. is the prayer of your unworthy brother.—D. J. Johns.

PREFACE

The "Preacher" has said, "Of making many books there is no end." The truthfulness of this statement is certainly verified in the minds of those who have had a glimpse of the endless lists of books of various kinds that have been published in the past and are offered for sale.

Regardless as to how bounteously the public and private libraries are supplied, there is always room for such volumes which, if carefully read, may prove helpful in bringing about better domestic, social, moral, and religious conditions in this world of sin.

The spirit of lawlessness in the State and Nation, the looseness of morals in society, the disloyalty in marriage relations, and the spirit of worldliness in many of the churches give positive evidence of a sad neglect of proper teaching and training in many homes of our socalled Christian nations.

The future well-being of the nation, the purity of society, the sacredness of the marriage relation, and the highest spiritual attainment of the Christian Church are all achievements which should be diligently sought for on the part of every Christian man and woman.

The Christian Home is the fundamental source of our national, social, moral, and spiritual well-being. Out of it will come the forces that will either strengthen or weaken the next generation and the generations to follow. This being true, it is very essential that from our homes shall go forth influences that are in the truest sense pure, true, honest, ennobling, unselfish, uplifting, and godly.

It is the sincere hope and prayer of the author that this small volume may prove helpful by way of inspiring its readers to become diligent in making its suggestions, admonitions, exhortations and teaching practical in every phase of the domestic life and thus, by the grace and help of God, bring about favorable results in moulding the lives and characters of those who in the future will take our place in the all-important work of extending Christ's cause and kingdom on earth, through diligent, loyal, devoted Christian service.

The Author.

CONTENTS

INTRODUCTORY

About three-quarters of a century ago an American traveler and poet died in Tunis, Africa, almost forgotten. Though consul at the time, he was buried in that far-off land, and for twenty-one years Africa was his grave.

But John Howard Payne had made his contribution to the world which has long secured for him a place in the affections of the music-loving world. Himself without a real home most of his life, this "aching void," no doubt added its touch of beauty to his world famous hymn beginning with the lines—

"'Mid pleasures and palaces, though we may roam,
Be it ever so humble, there's no place like Home."

This touching song had been sung into the hearts of so many people that finally a wealthy man, W. W. Corcoran of Washington, D. C., furnished the money needed to bring his body back to America, where in Oak Hill Cemetery near Washington his remains were laid to rest in 1873. "Home, Sweet Home," is the sweet refrain that has not only given Payne a world-wide fame but it has furnished the inspiration for thousands of others who were moved to nobler aspirations and better lives.

But the home of which John Howard Payne wrote is but an earthly type of a home more glorious

than anything this world has ever seen. When the
"Home, Sweet Home," of earth is coupled with the
eternal home in glory, it gives, it an added attraction
which only the heirs of the mansions in the skies
can appreciate. Hence the charm connected with
the inspiring message penned by another poet, David
Denham:

> "'Mid scenes of confusion and creature complaints,
> How sweet to my soul is communion with saints!
> To find at the banquet of mercy there's room,
> And feel in the presence of Jesus at home.
>   Home, home, sweet, sweet home,
>   Prepare me, dear Savior, for glory, my home.
>
> "I long, dearest Lord, in thy beauty to shine,
> No more as an exile in sorrow to pine,
> And in thy dear image arise from the tomb,
> With glorified millions to praise Thee at home.
>   Home, home, sweet, sweet home,
>   Prepare me, dear Savior, for glory, my home."

The Christian Home is a most fruitful place to
prepare young people for the trials and duties of an
earthly career which ends when the Master touches
them with the finger of death and bids them come to
the eternal Home above. No matter how precious
this place on earth may be, it can not mean all that
it should mean unless we look at this as but a temporary retreat until our Lord is ready to move us to
the mansions on high. To think of the eternal
Home gives the touch of sacredness to the home on
earth and makes us wish for the continual presence
of Christ in earthly homes. To this end parents,
children, and "strangers within the gates" should

do all in their power to make our present homes all that is possible for them to be in the way of headquarters for love and peace and righteousness and truth and happiness and serviceableness in the cause of Christ and the Church. It has well been said: "As is the Home, so is the community, the Church, the nation."

In the following chapters Brother Shoemaker discusses various phases and problems connected with the Christian Home, and offers practical suggestions for parents, children, servants, visitors, and everybody interested in the welfare of the Home. We are quite sure that if his instructions are heeded and his advice followed there will be a great uplift in many lives and homes. The many practical suggestions offered can not but be helpful to all sincere seekers after truth. And believing that you will be interested in the message that follows, I now lay down my pen after wishing the benediction of High Heaven to rest upon this effort on the part of our brother and subscribing myself,

Yours for happy, God-honoring Christian homes,

Daniel Kauffman.

A HOME POEM

Home is not simply a dwelling place,
  To keep one from the busy throng;
Nor haunt for one of the human race
  To indulge in things that are wrong.

It is not merely a boarding hall,
  Where families go to get their meals;
Nor is it the place to carry all
  The sad complaints and ills one feels;

Neither a building composed of walls
  That are beautified and gilded;
Home is a place where affection calls,
  And enjoys what love hath builded.

Home is not simply a living room,
  With nothing within to cheer it;
It is a place where sweet flowers bloom,
  And other things that endear it.

Home is love's treasure house complete,
  Where loved ones gather around the hearth;
It is a place to Christians more sweet,
  Than any spot on this cold earth.

Blessed indeed are the thoughts of Home,
  With its comforts and many joys,
From its realm there's no desire to roam,
  On the part of true girls and boys.

CHAPTER I

A PICTURE OF AN IDEAL CHRISTIAN HOME

> For I know him, that he will command his chil-
> dren and his household after him, and they shall
> keep the way of the Lord, to do justice and judg-
> ment; that the Lord may bring upon Abraham that
> which He hath spoken of him.—Gen. 18:19.

What was said of Abraham and the home he
had established should be said of every Christian
father and his home. If every home or household
were patterned after the aforesaid ideal home, this
world would be a paradise in comparison to what it
now is.

There are but few words in the English language that sound as musical to the ear and as
touching to the heart as the word **Home,** and there
is but one cther institution that is fraught with such
sacred memories to the Christian; namely, the Christian Church. Both the Home and the Church have
been divinely instituted. It is sad, however, to know
that both have been, in a general way, more or less
polluted through the influences of sin and disloyalty
to the principles which were divinely given to govern both institutions. The purity and sacredness of
the latter depends largely upon the purity, the loyalty, and the sacredness of the former. No human
being can estimate the far-reaching influences, either

for good or evil which have their origin in the institution called the Home.

The world's social, moral, and religious status, both in the past and present, give positive evidence that the homes in all ages and nations have been the moulders of character and the means of setting on foot certain agencies which have and are wielding a mighty power in the world, either in building up and exemplifying, or ignoring and destroying, the principles of righteousness in the nation, in the state, in society, and in the sacred institution called the Church. This being true, it should be the earnest aim and desire, also the fervent prayer, of every husband and wife, every father and mother, every member of the family circle to put forth the greatest possible effort to make their home-life truly ideal; that they through the providence of God and guidance of the Holy Spirit may be instrumental in bringing about a marked change for the better.

From observation we conclude that there is a vast difference in the minds of men and women as to what constitutes an ideal home. Many seem to have a false conception of true idealism in home-making. Grand architecture, elaborate furnishings and fine decorations, are usually considered the most essential in making a home ideal. Such ideals simply give evidence of worldly-mindedness rather than a true vision of the highest form of idealism; namely, the kind that brings real joy and happiness into the hearts and lives of those who (though living in an humble cottage) have enthroned Christ as the Head of their homes.

An ideal is that which is conceived to be perfect, or supremely excellent, or something very desirable. This should be the standard sought for in every home. The Christian Home is the only domicile that is in the truest sense ideal. It is not the display of art, wealth, splendor, or world grandeur that brings to the Home true joy, peace, happiness, contentment, and soul rest; but it is the abiding presence of Him who is the Author and Dispenser of all those valuable blessings, coupled with a devoted, self-sacrificing, sweet-tempered family group bound together with the cords of true love, that composes the crowning elements and supreme factors of a model Home.

Though one's earthly abode may be but a lowly cabin or humble cottage, located in a village or city or in a valley surrounded by hills and mountains or on the hillside or fertile plain, the same can be made an earthly paradise to a family in the truest sense if love is the ruling principle; parental and filial affection the uniting bond; truthfulness the basis of the conversation; cheerfulness the illuminating agency; virtue and chastity the code of morals; honesty and integrity the business standard; kindness, forbearance and self-sacrifice the factors used in calming troubled waters; faith, trust, and confidence the basic means of safe anchorage. These all coupled with true Christian piety and devotion are the great fundamentals and finishing touches of the ideal Home.

When we come in contact with individuals whose character and conduct in life are exemplary, it brings inspiration to us and proves to be an incentive to inspire one to live more nobly. The influence of one such life means untold blessings to others with whom it comes in contact. It is impossible for the human mind to grasp, and mortal tongue express, the great and lasting blessings which are being multiplied daily to humanity thru the influence and efforts put forth on the part of the many devoted and consecrated men and women who have been taught and trained for real usefulness in the various noble activities of life in true Christian homes, which in the past have been founded in various parts of the world.

A real Christian home is an earthly Eden in which all the beauties of the Christian religion with its fragrant blossoms of love, its delicious fruits of righteousness, and rich harvests of spiritual blessings are fostered, enjoyed, and perpetuated by those who live within its realm and strive to make their abode (by God's grace) a divine institution—a place where angels are pleased to hover over both day and night.

The Christian Home is typical of the New Jerusalem which John the beloved saw while in exile on the Isle of Patmos. It was a four-square city. Its length, breadth, and height were equal. The same is true of the Christian Home. Everything is established and carried on according to a four-square plan, exemplified in the relation of husband to wife, wife toward her husband, parents toward their children, and children toward their parents. The Holy City for which the Christian family is headed has twelve foundations, composed of stones exceedingly precious. This is also true of the Christian Home. It is founded upon twelve precious, indestructible, character-building principles; viz., love, peace, kindness, gentleness, forbearance, self-sacrifice, helpfulness, truthfulness, honesty, purity, devotion, and loyalty.

The benediction of heaven rests upon the consecrated family, the members of which are bound together with the bonds of true love and are laboring together diligently to make their home a training school in preparing the rising generation for real usefulness in the Lord's service, thus helping to extend His cause and kingdom at home and abroad, in whatsoever sphere the Lord through the Holy Spirit may direct.

We herewith present to the reader a number of inspiring thoughts gleaned from "The Royal Path of Life" which are indeed very timely:

"Home! how often we hear persons speak of the home of their childhood. Their minds seem to delight in dwelling upon recollections of joyous days spent beneath the parental roof, when their young and happy hearts were as light and free as the birds who made the woods resound with the melody of their cheerful voices. What a blessing it is, when weary with care and burdened with sorrow, to have a home to which we can go and there, in the midst of friends we love, forget our troubles and dwell in peace and quietness.

"Home! That name touches every fiber of the soul, and strikes every chord of the human heart with its angelic fingers. Nothing but death can break its spell. What tender associations are linked with home! What pleasing images and deep emotions it awakens! It calls up the fondest memories of life and opens in our nature the purest, deepest, richest gush of consecrated thought and feeling. Home is the chief school of human virtue. Its responsibilities, joys, sorrows, smiles, tears, hopes, and solicitudes form the chief interests of human life.

"There is nothing in the world that is so intimate and endearing as the relation of husband and wife; nothing so tender as that of children; nothing so lovely as that of brothers and sisters. The little circle is made one by a singular union of the affections. The only fountain in the wilderness of life, where man drinks of water totally unmixed with bitter ingredients, is that which gushes for him in the calm and shady recess of domestic life.

"Make a home; beautify and adorn it; cultivate all heavenly charms within it; sing sweet songs of love in it; bear your portion of toil, and pain, and sorrow in it; learn daily lessons of strength and patience there; shine like a star on the face of the darkest night over it, and tenderly rear the children the Lord shall give you in it. High on a pinnacle, above all earthly grandeur, all gaudy glitter, all fancied ambitions, set the home interests. Feed the mind in it; feed the soul in it; strengthen the love, and charity, and truth, and all holy and good things within its sacred walls."

Nothing on earth can excel the sublimity, affection, harmony, happiness, and quietness of a well governed home where love, joy, and peace exist in their fullness; a place where virtue is nourished, and every good trait of character and the principles of righteousness are fostered and exemplified.

The foregoing being true, oh! how desirous every Christian parent should be to make their home an ideal Christian institution, an abode where the spirit of our blessed Lord and Master is constantly manifested in the lives and conduct of every accountable member of the family.

Every Christian parent should say with Joshua: "As for me and my house, we will serve the Lord." All homes patterned after the Joshua type are divinely instituted, conscientiously governed, and wondrously blessed of the Lord both in time and eternity.

At this point the writer feels impressed to emphasize a few thoughts by way of repetition, in order to help the reader to more fully realize his or her sacred relation to other members of the family circle of which they are part. That they may be constrained through love to do their utmost, by the grace and help of our loving Lord, to faithfully perform their mission in the home:

1. May each reader recognize the fact that the true Christian Home is a mighty factor in producing things that are excellent, good, pure, and noble in the nation, state, society, and Church.

2. That the family circle, if based upon the principles of Christian love, devotion, and righteous-

ness, enjoys the most delightful, elevating, encouraging, and helpful relationship on earth.

3. As an institution the Christian Home is second to none in being a center of the purest affections and most desirable associations, if it is founded and governed according to the divine plan.

4. It is the sacred nursery and training school of the Christian Church in which the youthful generations are being taught, trained, and equipped for real usefulness in life and effective service for the Church.

We shall close this chapter with a number of Home Gems. In the following chapters it will be the aim of the writer to describe the relationship that should be sustained between each member of the family, and offer such suggestions as may prove helpful to the readers in making the homes of which they are members as near ideal as possible.

HOME GEMS

To Adam and Eve Paradise was Home. and to all the good and noble among their descendants, Home is Paradise.

*

There is no sanctuary more sacred, no institution fraught with greater responsibilities and vested with such momentous opportunities as the Home.

*

"When Home is ruled according to God's Word, angels might be asked to stay a night with us, and they would not find themselves out of their element."—**Spurgeon.**

*

The true Christian Home is God's flower garden in which the soil is enriched with love, the seed sown with carefulness, the plants watered daily with kindness, causing the buds to come forth at the proper time, opening into beautiful fragrant blossoms which enrich and beautify both earth and heaven.

*

"A Christian Home! What a power it is to the child when he is far away in the cold, tempting world, and voices of sin are filling its ears, and his feet stand on slippery places."—**Kittridge.**

*

Home is a real Eden to every member of the family circle which has its doors open to Christ and everything that is pure, true and uplifting to both mind and soul, and has closed its doors against Satan and everything that is corrupt, false, and destructive to character, morality, and Christianity.

*

The spirit and moral tone of the Home has untold influence on the youthful members of the family. If the home teaching is what it ought to be, its influence will fasten conviction on the young mind as to what is right and wrong, to the extent that the same can never be erased from the memory.

*

"It is to Jesus Christ we owe the truth, the purity, the warm affection, the holy aspiration, which go together in that endearing word—home; for it is He that has made obedience so beautiful, and affection so holy; it is He that has brought the Father's home so near, and has taught us that love is of God."—**Hamilton.**

*

The family group should ever keep their faces turned toward the Father's house, that the Home may ever be filled with the atmosphere of Heaven. Not only should the days begin and end with God, with memories appreciated and acknowledged, and sins confessed and forgiveness sought, but the divine presence should be the soul's chiefest joy and His glad service the soul's greatest delight.

*

"The sweetest type of heaven is Home—nay, Heaven is the home for whose acquisition we are to strive most strongly. Home, in one form or another, is the great object of life. It stands at the end of every day's labor and beckons us to its bosom, and life would be cheerless and meaningless did we not discern across the river that divides us from the life beyond, glimpses of the pleasant mansions prepared for us."—**Holland.**

*

"Our home joys are the most delightful earth affords, and the joy of parents in their children is the most holy joy of humanity. It makes their hearts pure and good, it lifts men up to their Father in heaven."—**Pestalozzi.**

*

"The domestic relations precede and, in our present existence, are worth more than all other social ties. They give the first throb to the heart and unseal the deep fountains of its love. Home is the chief school of human virtue. Its responsibilities, joys, sorrows, smiles, tears, hopes, and solicitudes form the chief interests of human life."—**Channing.**

*

"Six things are requisites to create a 'happy home.' Integrity must be the architect, and tidiness the upholsterer. It must be warmed by affection, lighted up with cheerfulness; and industry must be the ventilator, renewing the atmosphere and bringing in fresh salubrity day by day; while over all, as a protecting canopy and glory, nothing will suffice except the blessing of God."—**Hamilton.**

A VISION OF MARRIED LIFE

When two lives are linked as one,
  Bound together with sacred ties,
Then the pilgrimage has begun,
  Toward the Home beyond the skies.

The journey may be short or long,
  And strewn with thorns and flowers;
But if brightened with cheerful song,
  Happy and sweet will be the hours.

The fragrant flowers will ever bloom,
  Yes, all along the love-paved way;
Since lovers always do make room,
  For mutual joys, from day to day.

The cares of life become more sweet,
  When borne for those we truly love;
Briers seldom hinder the feet,
  In traveling toward the Home above.

When hearts and lives are truly one,
  In mutual joys, serene and whole;
The battles of life are easily won,
  Thru Him who keeps mind, heart, and soul.

Joys there are in such a union,
  That cannot be to others told;
It is a heart and soul communion,
  Which never, never can grow old.

CHAPTER II

MARRIAGE THE FUNDAMENTAL REQUIRE-
MENT IN ESTABLISHING A HOME

> God created man in His own image.....male
> and female created He them. And God blessed
> them, and God said unto them, Be fruitful, and mul-
> tiply, and replenish the earth, and subdue it.—Gen.
> 1:27, 28.

The scriptural, national, and municipal codes of
law clearly prove that marriage is both a divine and
civil institution. It stands first upon the list of divine institutions. God Himself instituted it as a
sacred relationship in the garden of Eden, for the
happiness of mankind and the perpetuity of the human race. Man was created in the image of God;
that is, in His likeness—not vested with His attri-
butes, but made in the likeness of Him in moral
qualities and perpetual existence. Hence man is
both morally and mentally a social being. This being true, "God said, it is not good that man should
be alone." Therefore God created for Adam a "help
meet for him," in the person of Eve, joined them
together in the bonds of holy matrimony, and placed
them in their beautiful Eden home, with the instructions "to dress it and to keep it," coupled with the
first positive command to "be fruitful, and multiply,
and replenish the earth." After the beautiful bridal

gift was presented to Adam, he gave expression to the following words of appreciation and welcome: "This is now bone of my bone and flesh of my flesh." It is well to note that he did not say, this is bone **like** my bone, and flesh **like** my flesh, but a part of his real self. Thus they sustained through life an inseparable relationship. What a perfect oneness the divine Creator has bestowed upon husband and wife! It is a blessing for which good men who dwell with their faithful, affectionate wives are ever filled with real gratitude toward Him who instituted the blessed nuptial tie, called marriage.

Of all strictly human relationships which are formed on earth and severed by death, whether sealed by a civil or religious ceremony, there is none as important and sacred as the marriage relation. It is a bond that has been divinely instituted for the happiness, comfort, moral advancement, perpetuation, and the best welfare of mankind.

Marriage imposes upon the contracting parties the most solemn obligations and duties in the establishing and building up of a model home. It is a union that surpasses in sacredness all other earthly relationships, in the work of character-moulding and safeguarding humanity against the influences of sin. Hence "for this cause shall a man leave his father and mother, and cleave to his wife."

Since the marriage relation is of such infinite importance, great care should be exercised in the selection of either husband or wife. Marriage being of divine origin, its rites and regulations are to be held sacred and inviolate in all ages, and in all generations of the human race, and no steps should be taken by any one to enter the bonds of matrimony until the question is definitely settled in the minds of the prospective bride and groom, that in taking such a step, it is for the best material, moral, and religious welfare of the contracting parties and their probable posterity.

Every one of marriageable age should remember that the relationship between husband and wife is not primarily secular, or sexual (though such a relationship, if the same is ordered according to God's plans is perfectly in order) but the primary object of the nuptial relationship should be to effect the highest mental, moral, and spiritual development, in properly teaching, training, and caring for the souls that through the providence of God may from time to time be added to the family group. The spiritual treasures that are brought into a home through the mating of two consecrated individuals, possibly followed by precious jewels called children, is infinitely more valuable than to be abundantly supplied with works of art, treasures of wealth, and other material things so highly valued by many who enter the marriage relation.

The married life, as God has planned it, should be the happiest, purest, fullest, richest, and most sa-

cred relationship in this life. It is God's ideal of
completeness. When God saw it was not good for
man to be alone, He caused Adam to be wrapped in
deep slumber, after which He gently removed from
his side sufficient material to create a woman, which
He presented to him to supply that which was lacking in his life; namely, that of a "help meet for
him"—not simply a **help eat,** as is the case in myr-
iads of homes in this present age. The words, "a
help meet," have a twofold signification; viz., a
help-mate (or real helper in the various phases of
their domestic life) and "A help **meet** for him;" that
is, a suitable helper, one who fills the bill as no one
else could.

It certainly was God's purpose in instituting
marriage that it should yield true happiness and add
to the fullness of both the physical and spiritual life
of both parties; that neither should be losers in their
marital relationship, but both be gainers. If in any
case marriage proves a failure in bringing blessings
to both husband and wife, in yielding real joy, or a
richer and fuller life, the fault cannot be with the institution, but on the part of one or both parties who
are bound together in the sacred contract, by failing
to fulfil, at least to a certain degree, the proper
marriage requirements.

The institution called marriage has not been de-
vised by any civil court, or any earthly law-giver,
but by the Omniscient God who placed the stamp of

His divine ordination upon it. This being true, how necessary it is for all who contemplate entering the sacred portals of marriage to very thoughtfully and prayerfully consider the sacredness, solemn responsibilities, and the momentous consequences which follow in its wake!

The marriage relation is the closest and most vital relationship on earth. Through its agency the earth is populated; home-making perpetuated; marital, parental, and filial love engendered; affection mutually manifested; social problems solved; the principles of righteousness instilled into the minds and hearts of the rising generation; right standards of frugality, economy, honesty and integrity established, and the doctrines and principles of the true Christian religion taught and exemplified by those who have seriously and prayerfully entered its portals. All these invaluable characteristic qualities are involved in the nuptial vow, after the officiating clergyman has said: "In the name of the Triune God, I declare you to be husband and wife."

It is certainly all important that prospective husbands and wives, who are considering the matter of choosing a life companion, look not so much to beauty, riches, socal polish, and fine equipment; but more especially to beauty of character, riches in home-making qualities, true soul polish, manifested in a disposition of kindness and cheerfulness, one who is clothed with the robes of purity and true

Christianity. These latter characteristics are infinitely more valuable than the former, and should be the ideals sought for in selecting a life companion.

There are certain relations that are unchaste and sinful and not scripturally permissible until after the marriage ceremony is performed. Chastity is one of the most valuable characteristics in the life of a lover. This being true, every young man and woman should guard with special care their virtue, that no reflection may rest upon either one after they are married and brought into such a kinship with each other in which it should be their highest aim to live for each other's best interests, which can only be done if their characters have been kept without a blot of sexual impurity or immorality while in an unmarried state.

Our Lord has said "What therefore God hath joined together, let not man put asunder." It is thus made clear that marriage is a sacred institution, divinely ordained to be indissoluble except by death. Nevertheless, in case of sexual infidelity on the part of the husband or wife, or if the marital relations are as described in I Cor. 7:15, there may be a separation without violating God's Word.

When two persons stand with clasped hands and united hearts before the marriage altar and solemnly promise before God and the witnesses present to take each other as husband and wife and to love, keep, and cherish each other until death, and the vow is kept sacred, only death can annul the relationship.

In considering the sacredness and insolubleness of the marriage relation, and the many sacred and far-reaching interests that are involved in such a bond, it is indeed timely to urge that the greatest care be taken before the betrothal is made that both parties may be confident that when the union is culminated it will prove to be a congenial one.

It is very evident from observation, that if there were more wisdom and prudence exercised, and forethought given in regard to marriage and its experiences, requirements, and results—on the part of those who take its solemn vows—there would be much less afterthought or regret, also much less remorse.

Our Lord and Master clearly defined the marriage relation and placed His sanction upon it as a divine institution by performing His first miracle as a wedding guest at Cana of Galilee. He also declared that there is but one just cause for separation prior to death. (See Matt. 5:27,28,32; 19:9.) He followed with the injunction that no scriptural license is given for remarriage on the part of those who are thus separated. Note what He says in Mark 10:11, 12: "Whosoever shall put away his wife, and marry another, committeth adultery against her. And if a woman shall put away her husband, and be married to another, she committeth adultery."

All such marriage relations are of an adulterous nature, and those who live a continuous adulterous life have no scriptural passport to be present at the "Marriage supper of the Lamb" (Rev. 19:9).

We are made to conclude from the reports that come to us both verbally and through the various present day secular and religious publications, that the human race is in a very demoralized condition with its multi-million divorce cases, its immoral status of society, its many political scandals, its commercial dishonesty, its deceptive teaching of science "falsely so called," its soul-destroying influences of vice and debauchery, and its "underworld" conditions in families. These sad conditions which are so manifest in this present age give positive evidence of awful failures made, on the part of multiplied millions, in the choosing of life companions and establishing domiciles which have proved to be but institutions of vice, debauchery, and sin of almost every description.

When marriage is "in the Lord," as God designed that it should be, the atmosphere of the home-life will be congenial, the domestic affairs will be well ordered, the spirit of love, sympathy, forbearance, patience and helpfulness will be daily manifested, and true Christianity will be the crowning characteristic used in completing the Home structure.

Suggestions To The Unmarried

Young man, before you begin some girl to **woo**, consider seriously what it may mean by the time you get **through**.

In contemplating courtship, be sure to thoughtfully and prayerfully consider what may be the possible outcome of such a relationship.

If you desire your marriage to be truly happy, and the future of your nuptial relationship prove a blessing to yourselves and others, the nature of your courtship must be pure, and mutually helpful and inspiring.

Be sure to remember that, in order to keep one's reputation unquestionable and the character unsullied, it is necessary to avoid late hours, lustful embraces, and unnecessary privacy during courtship.

Do not allow your courtship to be of the dreamy kind which may culminate in the kind of a marriage that will cause you to awake later on with a realization of sorrow and sad disappointment.

Courtship is the stairway by which lovers either ascend to a joyful marriage, crowned with a happy home and sweet family ties, or descend to a disappointed, unhappy, and sometimes unholy relationship which death alone can scripturally annul.

In choosing a life companion do not fail to consider the past heritage, the present character, and the real domestic worth of your prospective life partner.

As a young man, do not allow anything of an artificial nature—such as powder, paint, or any other beautifying touches that may be applied to the face or body—ever tempt you to become attached to one of the opposite sex.

Young man, if you are desirous of establishing a real home-like home, do not think of marrying a girl, even though she is exceptionally attractive in her appearance, if she is inclined to be unkind or disobedient to her mother, or fails to take any interest in household duties, or lacks the characteristics of being industrious and economical.

Young maiden, if you find that your suitor fails to have the necessary qualifications and characteristics to make married life and home-making agreeable, do not accept his proposal for marriage for fear it will be your last chance. It is infinitely better to be a left-over jewel, than to be the slave of an unworthy, beastly husband.

Though a young man's character may be in many respects commendable, nevertheless, if he is addicted to certain filthy or evil habits, do not think of marrying him, unless he is willing to deny himself of all such habits for your sake before the betrothal takes place.

Do not give your consent to marry any one whose life is questionable, with the expectation of reforming such an one after the nuptial knot is tied. As a rule, most of such endeavors are a failure, because the evils which have not been discarded before the marriage vows are taken become more aggravated when bound up with the matrimonial bond.

When contemplating courtship, betrothal, and marriage, do not permit physical attractions—such as beauty of face and features, graceful poise and manners, mental and social acquirements, fine equipage and artistic accomplishments, etc.,—to lure you to take even the first step toward the final goal called marriage, unless the one thus described is also in possession of a noble character; a congenial disposition, and is morally pure, strictly honest, and worthy of your marital companionship.

If you are blessed with a Christian father or mother, or both, it is well to ask them for counsel when considering either the matter of your courtship, engagement, or marriage. Having gone through that experience, they should be in a position to give helpful advice.

Do not as a Christian think of courting, and much less think of becoming the fiance, and later marrying one who is an unbeliever or non-Christian, because the same would be an unequal yoking together, hence unscriptural. Such unions usually prove very unsatisfactory and frequently end disastrously in leading the believing one to lose out spiritually.

MATRIMONIAL GEMS

Of all earthly **goods,** the best to be had is a **good** husband, or a **good** wife.

*

Men should keep their eyes wide open when contemplating marriage, but after marriage they should keep them closed to the wife's imperfections, providing she has any.

*

Those who choose a wife, should do so with the same care that a sensible prospective bride selects her wedding gown, being sure to select material with good wearing qualities.

*

One should never marry except for love, but it is the part of wisdom not to fall in love with anyone except with such an one as is enriched with a lovely character.

*

There can be permanent happiness in the married life, only to the extent that each party in turn is willing to give up his or her uncongenial traits of character and whimsical notions.

*

In choosing a wife as a life companion it is essential not only to think of one's self in reference to the pleasure of being daily associated with one of a social and congenial disposition, but forethought should be given relative to the best welfare of those who through God's providence may be brought into the home through her as a mother, lest a reproach come upon your posterity because of an evil heritage.

*

"Happy and thrice happy are they who enjoy an uninterrupted union, and whose love, unbroken by any complaints, shall not be dissolved until the last day."—**Horace.**

*

The married relation is incomplete if those wedded together as husband and wife fail to be united and blended together on every point. This can only be secured by making every interest common to both, their hearts throbbing with the same joys and sharing each other's pangs of sorrow, each cheerfully helping to carry the other's burdens.

"Marriage has in it less of beauty, but more of safety, than the single life; it hath not more ease, but less danger; it is more merry and more sad; it is fuller of sorrows and fuller of joys; it lies under more burdens, but is surrounded by all the strength of love and charity; and these burdens are all delightful."—**Jeremy Taylor.**

*

"The persons who have chosen each other out of all the species with the design to be each other's mutual comfort and entertainment have, in that action, bound themselves to be good-humored, affable, discrete, forgiving, patient, and joyful, with respect to each other's frailties and imperfections to the end of their lives."—**Addison.**

*

We entreat you as a husband to love your wife as you love yourself; yea, "even as Christ also loved the church, and gave himself for it." Give honor to her as to the more delicate vessel. Respect the delicacy of her general makeup, and ever protect her as a sacred treasure. Continue to manifest toward her through life the same attention, the same manly tenderness which in youth was the means of gaining her affections. Pursuing such a course will go a long ways in making your home ideal.

*

We exhort you as a wife to be gentle, kind, and obedient to your husband. May the influence which you wield over him arise from the discretion of your Christian conduct toward him. "Submit yourselves unto your own husbands, as unto the Lord." Be diligent in ornamenting your life with meekness, cheerfulness, and kindness, thus making yourself attractive to him to whom you have pledged faithfulness and loyalty.

*

Both husband and wife should constantly endeavor to preserve a strict guard over their tongues, that they never utter anything that is rude, contemptuous, or harsh; guarding well their tempers, that they may never appear sullen and severe; each endeavoring by God's grace to be as perfect as possible, but never expecting too much from each other. If perchance mistakes occur and offenses arise, the spirit of forbearance and forgiveness needs to be exercised, and the thought entertained that no human being is exempt from faults.

THE BLENDED LIVES

When two lives are blended,
As God hath intended,
Nothing can disturb their peace.
In each other confiding,
Their love is abiding,
And continues to glow and increase.

Clouds may darken the day,
And thorns found in the way,
While traveling the marital road;
But love with its strong arm,
Keeping its subjects from harm,
Will remove every burdensome load.

With hearts beating as one,
Nothing under the sun,
Can mar their pilgrimage thru life.
Because love, joy and peace,
Continues to increase,
Between them as husband and wife.

With the sunshine of good cheer,
The skies will be kept clear
From all that would tempt or annoy;
And through God's saving grace,
At the end of love's race,
The glories of heaven they'll enjoy.

CHAPTER III

THE RELATIONSHIP BETWEEN HUSBAND AND WIFE

> From the beginning of the creation God made them male and female. For this cause shall a man leave his father and mother, and cleave to his wife; and they twain shall be one flesh: so then they are no more twain, but one flesh. What therefore God hath joined together, let not man put asunder.— Mark 10:6-9.

These are the words of our Lord and Master, spoken to the Pharisees in answer to the question asked by them as to whether it was "lawful for a man to put away his wife." Our Lord's answer very vividly portrays the sacred and inseparable relationship which exists between husband and wife. It is well to note the four points in the divine order of the creation of Adam and Eve and their relation together as husband and wife:

1. God created them male and female—simply one man and one woman, thus clearly intimating that Adam was not to have a plurality of wives, neither have the opportunity to put away Eve and marry another.

2. The leaving of father and mother indicates that the ties which bind husband and wife together as one body, are more intimate and sacred than the ties between parents and children. The same proves

very clearly the nearness, and the perpetuity of the marriage relation.

3. The unity of the marriage relation is such that (though the contracting parties are two distinct individuals) they are **one flesh,** the uniting of two halves into one complete whole. The union between them is the most intimate and sacred of any relationship that can exist in this world, and if the nuptial vows are kept inviolate, as God intended that they should be, death alone can dissolve the sacred union.

4. That which God hath joined together is not to be severed by any human agency. Therefore, since marriage as an institution is sacred, and divinely ordered to be for life, He alone has reserved the right to sever this sacred earthly relationship, and that by the hand of death. He who created husband and wife to be real helpers suitable to each other, has in His infinite wisdom and goodness divinely ordered that those who are joined together in holy wedlock should live together in love and unity until death parts them asunder.

The relationship of husband and wife being so sacred, and its ties inseparable except by death, each should aim and earnestly endeavor to make the domestic life truly congenial, cheerful, happy, helpful, comfortable, encouraging, and in every respect ideal. This can only be done by guarding against and eliminating the evil tendencies of human nature and its out-croppings—such as thoughtlessness, indifference, selfishness, recklessness, waywardness, obstinacy, harshness, unkindness, and lustfulness—all of which are of a cankerous nature, and if tolerated in one's domestic life will destroy the purity, congeniality, and sanctity of the home life. Instead of tolerating and harboring the afore mentioned enemies in the family camp, both husband and wife should at all times put forth prayerful effort to exercise toward each other the spirit of true love, kindness, patience, forbearance, forgiveness, confidence, and mutual helpfulness. In so doing their relationship will in the truest sense be ideal.

Every husband and wife whom God has joined together in the sacred bonds of matrimony should seek by divine grace to make their relation to one another such as will meet with the approval of Him who is the founder of the marriage institution. Each should carefully and prayerfully consider how they should conduct themselves toward each other in their domestic life, and should earnestly endeavor to bring sunshine into each other's lives, thus filling each other's hearts with real joy and happiness, and furnishing the domicile with true peace and real comfort.

The relationship which is sustained between husband and wife is of a fourfold nature; viz., physical, mental, social, and spiritual. If the marital relation is to be ideal, as God designed that it should be, it is necessary that there be a perfect blending in those four points. This in most instances takes careful thought, prayerful endeavor, and divine help. The carrying out of the divine plan in the domestic life should be the constant aim of both husband and wife. This much desired goal may be reached by pursuing the following course:

1. The blending of their physical relation should be mutual in making the same helpful and agreeable to each other and fruitful in posterity.

2. Their minds should be amicably blended to the extent that it can be truthfully said of the nuptial pair that they are of one mind in their varied relationship—one in purpose, one in home ideals, one in aiming to attain to the noblest standards of life, and one in the Christian faith.

3. The social blending should not only determine the relation which should be sustained by each other in the Home, but towards those that are without its portals; also how to manifest the spirit of kindness, courtesy, and love for one another at all times.

4. The most sacred blending is that which has the effect of binding husband and wife together in an inseparable bond of Christian fellowship, unity of faith, and practice every day in the year until the end of life's pilgrimage.

To bring about these conditions in the domestic circle, which are of inestimable value to every member of the family and also to the Church, the state, and the nation, it is necessary on the part of both husband and wife to exercise the spirit of self-sacrifice, patience, forbearance, and courtesy.

One of the first lessons that need to be learned and practiced on the part of the nuptial pair is the spirit of self-sacrifice or self-denial. There are comparatively few husbands and wives that are exactly alike in their mental, social, and moral makeup, and are of such an even temperament that there is a perfect blending in every phase of their domestic life; hence it is usually necessary for those who have taken the sacred marriage vow to constantly manifest the spirit of sacrifice, ever seeking in a tactful way to be helpful in bearing one another's burdens along every line in their domestic relationship.

Oh, how the loving wife, who is sometimes cumbered with various household duties, is greatly cheered by the sacrifices made on the part of her husband in helping to lighten her burdens in the family circle; and vice versa, the acts of self-denial performed on the part of the wife to lighten her husband's burdens helps wonderfully in smoothing life's rugged pathway!

The lesson of patience and forbearance toward each other also needs to be learned and made practical if the relationship is to be congenial and ideal. Sometimes it takes considerable time to bring two lives into a perfect union, so that they blend in a loving way in every chord and tone. No matter how intimate and congenial the relations may have been before the marriage ceremony was performed, neither party has known perfectly the real life and character of the other until they have, at least for a season, traveled the connubial highway of life together; hence in all probability, after a certain period of time, both husband and wife may detect in each other certain characteristics which may not be very congenial and helpful in making the home life ideal. When such conditions become manifest it is the part of wisdom that both parties mutually agree to adapt themselves to the situation, and if possible decide upon some plan by which they may be able to counteract as much as possible all such unfavorable features that have a tendency to mar the peace and happiness of the home life.

At this point we shall refer to a narrative which came to our notice some years ago. The same may seem somewhat amusing, but it clearly portrays the point we wish to make. A certain husband and wife, whose given names were said to be John and Mary, had been happily married and loved each other sincerely. John worked in the shop and Mary his wife looked after the household duties. Occasionally things failed to move along smoothly, both in the shop and in the home, and as a result they would allow themselves to become somewhat irritated; and sometimes unkind words would be spoken, resulting in what might be termed a lover's quarrel. This had the effect of causing their domestic life to be more or less ruffled, which they both greatly regretted after the troubled waters were again calmed. One day after having passed through an experience of this kind, John and Mary talked the matter over in a kind and loving way, each giving evidence that they truly loved each other; and this being true they mutually decided to make an earnest endeavor to refrain from speaking harshly or unkindly to each other, after which John proposed that they mutually adopt a plan by which they might be enabled to avoid such unpleasant experiences, whereupon the following plan was agreed upon: John said, "When things go wrong in the shop during the day and I become somewhat irritated, and am still somewhat ruffled when I return for my meals, or after closing the shop for the day, I will have my hat placed on one side of my head, which will be an indication that my temper is not sweet; and when you see me coming with my hat tipped to one side, you simply meet me with a smile and treat me very kindly and all will end well. On the other hand if things go topsy-turvy in the home during the day and your temper is on tension, simply pin up the corner of your apron and when I come home anytime during the day and see the corner of your apron pinned up, I shall greet you with a smile and manifest a very friendly spirit, and thus we shall avoid a clash of words." The plan was adopted and worked splendidly from day to day. But one day conditions were woefully abnormal in the shop, to such an extent that when John left for his home he found it necessary to place his hat on the side of his head. When he arrived at his home and opened the door, he was met by his spouse with the corner of her apron pinned up. Now what was to be done? The situation seemed serious and quite embarrassing to both John and Mary. They looked at each other for a few moments in silence, after which they both began to smile, followed with a loving embrace, and it is said that that evening was the most pleasant they had spent together for some time. It is said that the plan was effective in bringing about a permanent remedy for the restoration of a congenial home life.

Another valuable quality that leads to happiness between husband and wife is genuine courtesy. This is usually very manifest during the season of courtship, which is perfectly right, but for some reason these very commendable civilities are sometimes dispensed with after the marriage vow has been taken. The smiles, kind words, and "thank you's," are in many cases to a greater or lesser degree either thoughtlessly or intentionally eliminated from the domestic life. Those civilities are usually extended to friends, neighbors, and the outside world, though in many instances they are not as deserving of the spirit of politeness and courtesy as are those who are bound together in the sacred nuptial ties. There is no place where discourtesy and rudeness are so unbecoming and out of place as in the domestic circle.

There is no place in all the world where courtesy should be as freely manifested as in the Home, between husband and wife, and parents and children. In the family group is where expressions of affection should be freely spoken and manifested in pure caresses. The domestic circle should at all times be a store-house of true love and courtesy. No earthly gifts can atone for the spirit of love and tenderness which may be lacking in the Home. Between husband and wife should ever be cherished, without any break whatever, the most complete courtesy, the kindest attention, the utmost regard, and the most unselfish civility that can be mutually expressed.

To crown the wedded life with the choicest of blessings, it is absolutely necessary to enthrone Christ in the Home and look to Him daily for His blessed benediction on the wedded life. Without the divine blessing being showered upon the lives of husband and wife, all the beauty of architecture, perfectness of furnishings, riches of earthly stores, domestic affection, and other temporary treasures cannot perfectly satisfy their hungry hearts and fill the same with fullness of joy and peace which may not for a moment be broken. The fullness of joy, peace, and love can only be realized in the truest sense when our precious Lord is crowned as Head of the institution called Home.

The responsibilities are too great, and the interests too precious, to venture into a marital partnership without the abiding Christ. His constant presence is needed as Savior, Teacher, Helper, and Comforter to save, teach, help, direct, console, and smooth life's pathway for those who are traveling together as husband and wife toward the Celestial City.

CONJUGAL GEMS

By careful procedure after marriage, the different characteristics of husband and wife may be made to produce a beautiful, harmonious combination of noble Christian qualities.

*

If husband and wife are to be truly happy in their domestic life, they will need to be mutually honest, chaste, and true.

*

Love is the dawn of marriage, and marriage, if ordered according to God's direction, is the zenith of true love.

*

When two individuals are properly mated, marriage to them is a sacred bond; but if the mating is such that their lives fail to become blended together in the bond of true love, their marriage relation becomes a state of bondage.

*

Husband and wife should not only endeavor to make their conjugal relation the "banqueting house" of love, but also the mutual paradise of courtesy and bond of domestic service.

*

When man and woman become united together in the bonds of matrimony, the imaginary ideals which they previously saw in each other's lives usually take wings and fly away; but the real traits of character are seen, and remain to mould the home life.

*

The happiness of the wedded life will depend largely upon the willingness of both husband and wife to make sacrifices for each other with readiness and real cheerfulness.

*

The paramount aim on the part of both husband and wife should be to work for a harmonious blending of their lives. Even though there are certain characteristics in each which may seem uncongenial to the other, there should be a loving endeavor on the part of each to supply the one thing needful to heal and cover the defects which may be more or less noticeable in each other's lives, and thus effect a perfect fusion of the two lives into one that is complete and indissoluble.

*

To enjoy a lasting unity in the matrimonial relation there needs to be a triune fellowship permanently established between the nuptial pair; viz., mind, heart, and soul fellowship—being of one mind in all their domestic problems and affairs, their hearts being bound together with the insoluble chords of love and sweet communion and actuated by true soul devotion and rendering loving service both to one another and to the Lord their Savior as Guide and Keeper.

THE HUSBAND'S MISSION

Through inspiration it is said,
That man is the woman's head,
Appointed of God to meet her needs.
Hence it should be his chief desire
To be her every need supplier,
And please her with his loving deeds.

His love to her should be complete,
Expressed in actions pure and sweet,
While trav'ling the marriage route together.
There should always be an overflow
Of joy and peace, as they onward go
Tho' sometimes meeting with stormy weather.

The husband should be good and true
To his dear wife, to whom is due
His constant love and tend'rest care.
And it should ever be his aim
To shield her from all harm and blame,
And for her good no effort spare.

When through love the bond is sealed,
It is to both a sacred shield
To ward off the things that sadly mar.
It is the constraining power within,
That gains the victory over sin,
And is to both life's guiding star.

CHAPTER IV

THE HUSBAND'S DOMESTIC COMMISSION

> The husband is the head of the wife, even as
> Christ is the head of the church.....Husbands, love
> your wives, even as Christ loved the church, and
> gave himself for it.—Eph. 5:23-25.

For reasons best known to himself and his Lord,
the apostle Paul chose to remain unmarried, hence
he knew not from experience how much is involved
in the marital relation. But through divine illumi-
nation he had a perfect conception of the sacred relationship that should at all times be sustained between husband and wife, parents and children, servants and their masters, and he also knew how to
rightly solve such problems which vitally effect the
lives of those who are bound together in family ties.

In his touching and very instructive epistle to
the believers at Ephesus, he clearly shows that the
husband sustains the same relation to his wife that
Christ does to the Church; viz., that the husband
has been divinely designated as the head of the wife.
This does not imply that the husband is to rule over
his wife as an austere judge or king, but in the same
manner as Christ is the governing head of the
Church. Christ being the Head of the Church, He
is its spiritual director and moulding power. In

reference to the headship in the domestic circle, the same is vested in the husband, providing all things are normal in the qualifications and characteristics of husband and wife.

God said to Mother Eve after the fall: "Thy desire shall be to thy husband, and he shall rule over thee." The ruling was not to be with a rod of iron, or in the spirit of severity, but with the scepter of love, as embodied in the Golden Rule. Eve being a part of Adam's flesh and bone, taken out of his side, she was to lovingly and submissively stand by his side, close to his heart; and he as her head to be her counselor, keeper, and director in their domestic life.

The domestic relation between husband and wife is strikingly portrayed in the divine relation which is sustained between Christ and His Church of which He is the Head.

As the brain or head of the individual suggests and dictates to the various members of the body, there is a prompt response without any hesitation, to move, act, and perform according as has been suggested by the head, and all working in ready co operation for the satisfaction and best interests of both the body and mind, or head. Thus all the members of the body work together conjointly, providing the entire body is in a normal condition and able to function aright. The same is true of the Christian church in its relation to Christ as its head.

Christ, the Head of the Church, simply inspires, suggests, and dictates to each corporeal or actual member of His body, the Church, and there is a prompt and loving response on the part of each member to do the things which will bring joy, peace and happiness to both the Church as a Body and to Christ its Head. In a similar way, the husband as the head of the wife is the suggestive, directive, and governing authority in the home, and his mission is to so order the affairs of their domestic life that the best interests of both will be served, both for time and eternity. If on the part of the wife there is a cheerful, loving, and prompt reciprocation in helping the husband to carry out his sacred commission in the home, the same will be to them and others a real paradise.

Paul also clearly portrays to us the measure of the love that husbands are to have toward their wives. No human being is able to fathom the depth of Christ's love for His Church, and in comparing man's finite love with the infinite love of Christ we are made to see that no one can love to the same degree that Christ loved His Bride, the Church, in giving Himself a ransom for it. Nevertheless, it is clearly implied in Paul's inspired statement that the husband through the spirit of self-sacrifice and self-abandonment is to manifest toward his wife whole-hearted devotion, thus giving himself for her best physical, moral, and spiritual interests.

The devoted husband who truly realizes all that is involved in this divine command readily closes his heart against all selfishness and everything that would bring grief to the heart and life of his "better half." He is not so much concerned about his own comfort, but the one thing paramount in his mind is how he may be able to help and make things congenial and comfortable for his wife. He is diligent in his toils from day to day that he may be able to amply support her, and provide for all her needs. He is willing to deprive himself of certain comforts in order to shelter her from the storms of life; in fact, he counts no sacrifice too great to be made for her benefit. Nothing less than this can be implied in loving one's wife as Christ loved His Church and gave Himself for it.

Such self-denying love manifests itself in true affection and the utmost gentleness in speech and actions, which has a wonderful effect in satisfying the heart of a loving wife. Husbands should not hate, or scold, or chide, or illtreat their wives at any time or in any way. Neither should they simply manifest their love by smiles, caresses, kind words, or by gifts, and the needed support: but their love should ever be of a sacrificial nature, manifested constantly in making self-denials, assisting in household duties, abstaining from useless and filthy habits, and cheerfully helping to lighten all domestic burdens—and thus give evidence to the wife and others who may be within the domestic circle that pure, ardent, salf-sacrificing, Christ-like love is th constraining power within the heart.

The same apostle, in his epistle to the believers at Colosse, said: "Husbands, love your wives, and be not bitter against them." All display of ill temper is to be carefully guarded against on the part of the husband, whether it is manifested in bitter feelings, or in unkind actions and angry words. Being conscious of the fact that human nature is easily ruffled and provoked to the extent that unkind words are apt to be spoken in an unguarded moment, which may quench the flame of love in the heart of the faithful wife, it should ever be the sacred duty of the husband to prayerfully suppress all bitterness in the heart, asking the Lord for the needed grace to change the ruffled feelings into sweet calmness and tender affection.

It is a lamentable fact that many married men, and some of them claiming to be Christian husbands, are courteous, polite and kind toward those who are without the pales of the home, but have fallen into careless and rude habits in the domestic circle, such as being unsocial, sullen, careless in speech, easily provoked, irritable, heedless as to the nature of their conduct, and indifferent to the wife's wishes, ideals and needs. Such conduct may be unintentional on the part of the husband, thinking that because a woman is his wife she should understand him, and should not question his love toward her, even if he is rude, and sullen, and unsocial toward her much of the time. This is indeed a false and sinful attitude for any man to take toward his wife, whom he has solemnly promised to love, cherish, protect, and support as long as they both shall live. There is no other woman in all the world that so keenly feels the sting of harsh expressions and unkind actions as the one to whom he, as a husband, has pledged his love and devotion. And truly there is no other whose feelings he should be more careful not to hurt or grieve. Neither the divine law, nor the marriage vow, nor true love, give any license for incivility or rudeness toward the one who is to be truly loved and cared for by her husband.

A certain author very touchingly describes how the husband should sympathetically enter into the trials confronting his wife, as follows: "While gentleness should always mark a husband's bearing toward his wife, there are occasions which call for peculiar thoughtfulness and sympathetic expression. Sometimes she is weary. The cares of the day have been unusually trying. Matters have not gone smoothly at home. Her quivering nerves have been sorely overtaxed. She has heard sad news. A child has been sick all day, or, worse still, has by some disobedience or wrongdoing almost broken her heart. What is a husband's part at such times? Surely if he is capable of tenderness he will show it now. He will not utter a word to add to the load the overburdened spirit is already carrying. He will seek rather by every thoughtful help his love can give to lighten the burden, to quiet the trembling heart and to impart strength and peace."

• Every wife should have the assurance that she will always find in her husband a safe and quiet refuge when she is sorely tried and perplexed with life's problems and duties. Also being confident that he fully understands the longings of her heart, and will deal gently with her in times of trial and suffering, being willing to do all he possibly can to shield her from the storms of life, and give even his own life if need be to save hers. There should be no occasion for the wife to doubt her husband's willingness to stand by her in whatever way she may be tested and tried. No fear should at any time be entertained of being repulsed, or rebuked with coldness when she flees to him for succor and shelter.

The true husband will ever manifest great respect and regard for his faithful wife. He had confidence in her, and great respect for her before she became his bride. He seemed to see in her all that was pure, lovely, and noble; now since he has chosen her as his bosom companion, and considered her the most "precious among ten thousand," he certainly should not think of loving and respecting her less but should love her more and more as they travel together life's pilgrimage. Having been bound together by the most sacred ties on earth, there is abundant reason why their relation together as husband and wife should be the most congenial and happy of any human relationship.

The true husband will cheerfully seek to make his wife a mutual sharer of his own life along every line in which it is possible for him to do so. He will confide in her in every phase of their domestic life. He will counsel her in his business or professional affairs. He will consult her as to what steps should be taken when perplexing problems arise, either in or out of the home. Whether the day brings forth victory or defeat, success or failure, joy or sorrow, sunshine or shadows, he will confide all to his wife in the evening. He will, as much as possible, arrange to spend his evenings at home. He will assist the wife and mother in the teaching and training of the children entrusted in their care, if through the providence of God their home is blessed with such a rich heritage. He will be faithful in giving her all the encouragement he can in making their home a true Christian home, where Christ reigns supreme.

When a man and woman have joined hands and hearts in taking the marriage vow, they are linked together in the closest of all earthly ties. What concerns the one concerns the other. Their interests are one. Therefore the husband should make his

wife the intimate sharer of his entire life. No part
of it should be closed against her. She should share
his successes, victories and triumphs, and have the
privilege to rejoice with him in the same. If failures and reverses come to the husband, she should
be apprised of these, that she may be in position to
sympathize with him and lend such encouragement
as will help remove the clouds from the mental
horizon. Their lives having been linked together as
one, they should share each other's pains and trials
as well as the pleasures and comforts of married
life.

Dr. J. R. Miller, the author of the book entitled,
"The Home Beautiful," very aptly portrays the ideal relationship that should exist in every Christian
home, as follows: "Every true-hearted husband
seeks to be worthy of the wife he has already won.
For her sake he should reach out after the noblest
achievements and strive to attain to the loftiest
heights of character. To her he is the ideal of all
that is manly, and he should seek to become every
day more worthy of the homage she pays him. Every possibility in his soul should be developed. Every latent power and energy in his life should be
brought out. His hand should be trained under
love's inspiration to do its most skillful work. Every fault in his character should be eradicated, every
evil habit conquered, and every hidden beauty of
soul should burst into fragrant bloom for her sake

She looks to him as her ideal of manhood, and he must see to it that the ideal is never marred—that he never falls by an unworthy act of his own from the high pedestal in her heart to which she has raised him.   Among all sins few are worse than those by which a man draws down shame and reproach upon himself, for, besides all the sorrow he brings upon her in so many other ways, he thus crushes in his wife's heart the fair and noble image of manhood which she had enshrined there next to her Savior's."

DOMESTIC GEMS

The following gems accompanied with quotation marks are, as the above, credited to Dr. Miller:

*

"When man offers his hand in marriage to a woman he says by his act that his heart has made choice of her among all women; that he has for her a deeper and tenderer affection than for any other."

*

"There is something very sacred and almost awe-inspiring in the act by which a wife, at her entrance into the marriage state, confides all the interests of her life to the hands of him whom she accepts as her husband."

*

"It is a solemn thing for any man to assume such a trust and take a wife—a gentle, delicate, confiding young life—into his keeping, to shelter, to bless until death either takes the trust out of his hands or strikes him down."

*

"What Christ is to His people in their weariness, their sorrow, their pain, their alarm, every husband in his own little measure should be to his own wife."

*

"The husband who would have his wife's nature blossom out into its best possibilities of character, influence and power must make a genial summer atmosphere for his home all the year round."

*

"Husbands, love your wives." This is a command given by divine authority. The sentence is very short, but if fully accepted and observed on the part of the husband, in it is embodied the secret of real happiness and soul satisfaction, if coupled with the love and presence of Christ.

*

"It is a step in the right direction when a husband is not bitter against his wife, and it is a good deal farther in the right direction when, instead of being bitter, his words and acts and whole bearing are characterized by gentleness and affectionateness."

*

The husband's life, through true love, should be so interwoven with the heart and soul of his wife, that in the truest sense they are one in every phase of life—physically, morally, socially and religiously—working for each other's best interests both for time and eternity.

*

Great responsibilities and sacred duties are conferred upon every man who has pledged vows with a woman whom he has chosen from among all other women to be his wife. These solemn obligations and duties which he owes his wife can only be discharged by keeping perpetually in his mind the necessity of taking advantage of every passing opportunity to lend a helping hand in bringing into her life the richest treasures of his love, care, and sympathy.

*

Men often forget that they owe to their wives special duties. There is no man who has a faithful wife but owes her a debt he can never pay. She has given him a human heart, which is worth more than great wealth can purchase. In accepting his hand and heart she has paid him the greatest compliment that any human being can pay another. By leaving a loving father and mother she has clearly manifested that he is dearer to her than all other associations of her past life. For all this the husband should not fail to show his greatest appreciation for all she has sacrificed for his sake in becoming willing to become his wife and share with him life's joys and sorrows.

A GOOD WIFE, A VALUABLE TREASURE

There is nothing in this present life
  To be compared to a faithful wife.
In her true friendship and love combine
  To complete the bond which is divine.

Her life shines bright from day to day,
  Keeping her loved ones from going astray.
Her smiles bring joys within the Home,
  Curbing the desire from it to roam.

Her husband in her love confides,
  Because the same toward him abides;
Not simply during one short year,
  But until life is ended here.

It gives her joy her spouse to please,
  And ever keep his mind at ease;
When trials come and vex him sore,
  She seeks to cheer him more and more.

She is submissive to his will,
  And seeks his wishes to fulfil;
Knowing that it is of her required
  In the holy Book, by God inspired.

There is no sacrifice too great,
  For her to make for her dear mate
Whom she hath vowed to truly love
  Until they're called to heaven above.

CHAPTER V

THE WIFE'S DOMESTIC SPHERE

> Wives, submit yourselves unto your own husbands, as unto the Lord.....As the church is subject unto Christ, so let the wives be to their own husbands in everything.....And the wife see that she reverence her husband.—Eph. 5:22, 24, 33.

Since the marriage relation is so sacred, and the consequences which follow in its wake so far reaching, and the scriptural requirements relative to the institution so vital and momentous, it is highly essential for every unmarried woman, and girl of marriageable age, who may contemplate getting married, to consider very thoughtfully and prayerfully all that is involved in such a union before becoming betrothed and taking the final step in the sealing of the matrimonial bond.

Husband and wife have been divinely called to be one complete body, even as Christ and His Church are one body. If they in the truest sense sustain such a relationship, then their home will be a veritable paradise from which will go forth influences which will mean much in the way of bringing infinite blessings to themselves and their posterity, and others as years roll on.

In the preceding chapter we aimed to make clear the husband's relation to his wife as her head

and his commission as a unifying factor in the
home, basing our statements on Paul's version of an
ideal domestic relationship. In this chapter we shall,
from the same epistolary writings, show the relation
of the wife to her husband and her position and mission in the family domicile.

It is a divine requirement that wives be submissive to **their own** husbands (not to some one
else's husband, as the manner of some is) "as unto
the Lord." That is, as those who, in obeying their
husbands, are obeying the Lord Jesus, because He
requires of them such obedience as is in harmony
with His divine law. The inspired apostle clearly
shows that Christian wives are to pay all due respect, honor, subjection, and obedience to their own
husbands, who have by the marriage bond, devoted
themselves to their wives in accordance with the
divine arrangement. They should always so conduct
themselves as in the sight and presence of the Lord
Jesus Christ, with an eye single to God's glory.
The duty prescribed to wives is submission to their
husbands in the Lord, which means both to honor
and obey them "as it is fit in the Lord" (Col. 3:18).
This scripture makes it clear that such submission
is required of wives as will tend to Christ's and the
Father's glory. It is not to be understood that the
submission is to be arbitrary, or unlimited, nor of a
slavish kind whether in accordance to God's will or
not; but a loving submission that will in every way

possible prevent confusion, disorder, or anything that would have a tendency to mar the joy and peace of the divinely planned home life. The obedience that is enjoined upon the wife is that which is prompted by the principle of true love, both toward her husband and toward Christ the Lord. To do otherwise is to violate God's command, and thus fall under condemnation through disobedience.

Note further Paul's emphatic admonition, that "As the Church is subject to Christ, so let the wives be to their own husbands in everything." Since the true Christian Church (Christ's body) is cheerfully and faithfully subject to the authority of Christ in all its sacred work and spiritual relations, even so should all wives, with meekness, willingness and true fidelity, be subject to their own husbands in all things that are in accordance to God's will and Word. Since the inspired apostle was addressing believers only, it is to be understood that the obedience of the wife who is in the Lord, is that of obeying her husband who is also in the Lord. Obedience is excluded if the command given on the part of the husband is not in accordance with Christ's Word.

The wife is also to "see that she reverence her husband!" not in the same sense that she is to reverence God and the Lord Jesus Christ, but in a reverential way she is to honor her husband; respecting his authority as her head, and thus promote the peace, usefulness and happiness of the family relation. It is not only a wife's privilege, but her sacred duty (through divine guidance) to love, obey, and reverence her husband. To so order her household affairs, and make any such sacrifices at his request as may bring the greatest glory to God, and tend to the best interests of all who are members of the family.

If the nuptial relations are to be congenial in every respect, and the family interests are to prove a special blessing to all who are connected with the home, it is necessary that all members do their utmost to make their abode an earthly paradise where love reigns supreme, and righteousness predominates within its sacred realm.

In order to make the home complete and fill it with real refreshing influences, the same will need to be embellished with a loving Christian wife and mother. She is in the truest sense the key-stone which God uses to bind the domestic structure together, and make it an ideal resting place, and shelter in times of storm.

When a woman is chosen from among all other women to be the wife of a good, true, and noble man, she should manifest great respect to the one who has bestowed upon her the honor to be his life companion. He has been pleased to exalt her by enthroning her as the chief jewel of his heart and life. She has been chosen as the mistress of his domicile to beautify, brighten, and take care of the lovers' abode called home. To make it as far as possible, the most inviting, restful, comforting, and encouraging dwelling place in all the world, for all connected with the family.

Those who have not taken the final step of becoming the wife of some man, will do well to take time for serious thought and prayerful consideration before accepting a proposal of marriage, and thus ascertain what it may mean both to herself and others to give her hand and heart into the keeping of one of the opposite sex as long as both parties are permitted to live.

It should be definitely settled in the mind of every unmarried woman as to whether he who is paying attention to her is worthy of her confidence and the trust she is required to surrender to him for life. She should be assured that it will be his chief aim and purpose to bring true happiness into her life, and she should be certain that he is indeed worthy to be enthroned to the highest place in her human affections, and worthy to be respected and honored as a husband should be by a noble wife. It is highly essential that every unmarried maiden or woman consider seriously these vital questions before taking the nuptial vow, or she may learn when too late that he for whom she surrendered her all—and to whom she pledged her solemn promise to love, honor and obey—is far from being worthy

of the sacred trust which was committed to him, and
sadly fails in filling her life with joy and happiness
as had been expected on her part. Thus her heart's
desires and her soul needs are not being supplied as
they should be in their inseparable relationship as
husband and wife.

It is very essential that a wife be faithful to the
sacred charge committed to her in her domestic
sphere. This is very aptly portrayed by Dr. Miller,
as follows: "A true wife by her character and by her
conduct proves herself worthy of her husband's
trust. He has confidence in her affection; he knows
that her heart is unalterably true to him. He has
confidence in her management; he confides to her
the care of his household. He knows that she is
true to all his interests—that she is prudent and
wise, not wasteful nor extravagant. It is one of the
essential things in a true wife that her husband shall
be able to leave in her hands the management of all
domestic affairs, and know that they are safe. Wife-
ly thriftlessness and extravagance have destroyed
the happiness of many a household and wrecked
many a home. On the other hand, many a man
owes his prosperity to his wife's prudence and her
wise administration of household affairs. Every
true wife makes her husband's interests her own.
When burdens press upon him she tries to lighten
them by sympathy, by cheer, by the inspiration of
love. She is never a weight to drag him down, but

a real help to him along every line."

Christian wives will do well in their domestic
sphere, if they prayerfully study and carefully exemplify the injunction given by Paul in his epistle to
Titus (Chap. 2:4, 5). Paul, through divine inspiration, gives, especially to young wives, definite instructions as to how they shall conduct themselves
as wives and mothers. Note prayerfully what he
says. He instructs and encourages them to be prudent and carefully avoid everything that savors of
lightness or unchastity; to "love their husbands" and
children in an affectionate, endearing, and helpful
manner; "to be discreet," cautious, careful, and
obliging in their domestic relations; "chaste," quiet,
modest, and virtuous; "keepers at home," not spend-
ing their time in gadding about, and thus neglecting
their household duties, or doing as the same apostle
reports concerning widows who spent their time in
"wandering about from house to house," being
idlers, tattlers, and "busybodies, speaking things
which they ought not." The wife is divinely required (if conditions are normal) to "bear children,
guide the house, give none occasion to the adversary
to speak reproachfully" of the wife's attitude toward
her husband and home. She is to be industrious and
faithful to her trust as a housekeeper, and give careful attention to her husband and children as her sacred trust. She is also exhorted to be "good;" that
is, to be of a meek and humble spirit, and ever

ready to manifest a spirit of kindness, forbearance and helpfulness; like Dorcas, being "full of good works and alms deeds;" "obedient to their **own** husbands," lovingly rendering a submissive and obedient attitude toward them in everything that is scripturally lawful for them to do, "that the Word of God be not blasphemed," that is, that Christ and His Gospel be not reproached by encouraging disorderly conduct or practices in the home. Those wives who follow diligently the instructions given by Paul will by God's grace be enabled to faithfully fulfil their domestic sphere to the best interests of all connected with them in their homes by sacred family ties.

Too often when young men and women contemplate getting married, they think only of the desires of the flesh, and sadly ignore the need of considering the details and true ideals of house-keeping. Their connubial dreams are far from giving them a true vision of the essentials needed in making an ideal, happy home. The great essentials in real home-making, are, in the minds of many young people, simply commonplace things, not worthy to be considered. The mere thought, and much less the mentioning of such things as cooking, baking, dusting, sweeping, scrubbing, washing, ironing, and mending would be considered matters altogether unworthy to be taken into consideration when the question of marriage is discussed by certain lovers.

The qualifications necessary for good house-keeping and home-making are in many cases considered so insignificant and non-essential on the part of those who contemplate getting married that they fail to give the matter any thought as to whether the prospective wife will be able to faithfully and successfully perform her household duties to the extent that the meals, the home, and the atmosphere will be inviting to others who may come into the home either as visitors or by birth. The wife that can bake sweet light-bread, instead of bread that is sour and solid; or cook and season the food in a way that is palatable and much appreciated, instead of being scorched and void of the necessary seasoning; and prepare the meals regularly and on time, instead of scantily and tardily; also by diligent effort keeps the home neat, clean, and inviting, instead of having everything in a topsy-turvy style, coupled with unsanitary and repulsive conditions, is the wife that is infinitely more valuable than the one who for lack of qualifications and willingness fails to fill her mission in making her home and its furnishings inviting.

Those who so thoughtlessly enter the marriage relation are not long within the walls of their abode called Home, until they find to their sorrow that infinitely more is needed in the home equipage than a physically charming wife, if the home life is to be happy and made a success.

Undoubtedly many heart estrangements have had their origin in homes where the meals were served tardily and the food prepared poorly. Poor house-keeping, extravagance, untidiness and carelessness in general, on the part of the wife, will soon drive every vestige of attraction out of the Home. If she proves to be incompetent in the management of her domestic affairs, the wife will soon lose all the attractive features she may have appeared to have in the eyes of her husband. Good house-keeping is one of the most charming qualities of a good and noble wife.

A true, affectionate, scripturally submissive wife has the effect of making her husband's life more noble, stronger, and more perfect by her unselfish devotion to him as her head. While clinging to him in devoted confidence and loyal submission, she draws out of his heart and life the characteristics that are richest and noblest in his being. She inspires him with courage, loyalty, and faithfulness. She puts the beautifying touches on his life, and mellows him in whatever may have seemed to be rude, harsh, and unkind in his life by nature or disposition. She with her wise and pleasing methods moulds him into a model example of mankind. While she submissively yields to his counsels and instructions, she nevertheless, in her queenly way, leads him onward and upward in the path of rectitude and manly perfection.

No wife can meet the requirements of being an ideal home-maker unless she is a good woman, and she cannot in reality be a good woman unless she has accepted Christ as her Savior, and has become a true Christian wife. Nowhere except in the Lord Jesus Christ can she find the wisdom, the strength, and the beauty of character needed to meet the solemn and sacred responsibilities of true wifehood.

WIFELY GEMS

The foundation of true domestic happiness is centered in a virtuous, loving, devoted, industrious, sympathetic, congenial, faithful Christian wife.

*

Of all treasures that to man, by fortune's hand is given, the most precious and valuable is that of a devoted, loyal, faithful wife.

*

Of all earthly **goods** that God has given to man, the value of which cannot be estimated, is a truly **good** wife—and the bitterest experiences that a man can be made to endure and suffer, is in being bound for life to a worthless, depraved, and shiftless wife.

*

"A true wife gives her husband her fullest confidence. She hides nothing from him. She gives no pledges of secrecy which will seal her lips in his presence."

*

The true Christian wife and mother holds in her hand the scepter that under God's direction shapes the destinies of humanity, and moulds the character of the rising generation for real usefulness in life. This she does by instilling into their minds and hearts the soul-quickening principles of the Gospel.

*

A faithful wife will make her own home as near the ideal standard as it is possible for her to make it, rather than give her time to attend women's clubs, social betterment society meetings, home bureau meetings, and other such meetings the attending of which would lead to the neglect of home and family duties.

*

A wife's best home-making qualities are not to be found in a bright intellect, or in a graceful form and beauty of face, but in her womanly affections which minister refreshment of life to others, by her sympathies, rather than by her superior knowledge, or handsome face, or form.

*

A good wife is the highest, noblest and most precious gift to man. Her mission is to beautify the home with her smiles, courtesies, and sympathies, and enrich it with her labors of love and unselfish efforts in making it an ideal family domicile.

*

A noble wife is, next to salvation, heaven's best gift to man. She is to him a gem of many virtues. Her voice is the most enchanting music. Her smiles are more appreciated than sunshine. Her words are the guardian of her husband's manhood. Her prayers the assurance of his safety. Her industry the source of his success, and her heart and soul his greatest treasure.

*

"A good wife is like the ivy that beautifies the building to which it clings, twining its tendrils more lovingly as time converts the ancient edifice into a ruin."—**Johnson.**

*

"Save the love we pay to heaven, there is none purer, holier, than that a virtuous woman feels for him she would cleave to through life. Sisters part from sisters, brothers from brothers, children from their parents, but such a woman from the husband of her choice, never!"—**Knowles.**

*

"To be man's tender mate was woman born, and in obeying nature she best serves the purposes of heaven."—**Schiller.**

*

"The highest gift and favor of God is a pious, kind, godly, domestic wife, with whom thou mayest live peaceably, and to whom thou mayest entrust all thy possessions, yea, thy body and thy life."—**Luther.**

"A good wife makes the cares of the world sit easy, and adds a sweetness to its pleasures; she is a man's best companion in prosperity, and his best if not only friend in adversity; the most careful preserver of his health, and the kindest attendant in his sickness; a faithful adviser in distress, a comforter in affliction, and a discreet manager of all his domestic affairs."—**L. M. Stretch.**

*

"The good wife is generous and warm-hearted. She does not grow grasping and selfish. In her desire to economize and add to her stores she does not forget those about her who suffer want. While she gives her wisest and most earnest thought and her best and most skilled work to her own home, her heart does not grow cold toward those outside who need sympathy. A woman whose heart is not touched with the sight of sorrow, and whose hands do not go out in relief where it is in her power to help, lacks one of the elements which make the glory of womanhood."—**Dr. Miller.**

A TRIBUTE TO MOTHER

Within home's dear sacred walls,
Rich blessings did abound;
With mother's gentle calls,
Our hearts were made to bound.

There was no food more sweet,
Than mother's pie and cake;
She sure was hard to beat
In things that she did make.

Kind words and cheery smiles,
Our mother usually gave;
She smoothed the lonely miles,
By being kind and brave.

She brought to us good cheer,
When the sun failed to shine,
And always was so near
When darkness did entwine.

She gave us good advice,
And prayed for us, I know;
Making many a sacrifice,
Her love to us to show.

When you are old and gray,
And can but slowly walk,
You'll oft think of the day,
When you with mother could talk.

CHAPTER VI

THE PARENTS' RELATION TO THEIR CHILDREN

Train up a child in the way he should go; and when he is old, he will not depart from it.—Prov. 22:6.

Children are living jewels, given to parents by a loving Father who requires that they be properly taught and trained, that they may grow up a blessing to the present world and eventually shine with Him in the world to come.

Comparatively few parents realize the vital relationship which exists between them and their offspring, and fewer still are conscious of the great responsibilities which are resting upon them in the work of bringing up and training their children. The greatest mission that most parents can perform in the world is to rightly instruct their children, and train them for real usefulness in life.

The future of the state and Church depends largely upon the principles taught and instilled into the minds and hearts of the rising generation. This great work must necessarily be done by Christian parents in Christian homes. We tremble to think what may be the moral and religious condition of the world in the generations to come, if parents fail to give their children the proper training now.

The present day tendency, in regard to family life, is to indulge children rather than restrain them. Fathers and mothers, in these latter days of looseness and instability, are inclined to gratify almost every desire of their children rather than to deny them anything, even things that are positively harmful to both body and soul. In fact, children are practically taught self-gratification, rather than self-denial and submission to constituted authority, which are the first principles of the Christian religion and the prime means of juvenile character-moulding. Such indulgences on the part of the parents are certainly wrong. It is not only contrary to the teachings of Scripture, but it is sadly injurious to the best interests of the children, of society, and of the Church.

It is not only true that many parents sadly fail in teaching and training the children which, through the providence of God, have been entrusted into their care, but many husbands and wives deliberately close the doors of nature against the admission of children into their homes. Such a course is a violation of the divine command "to multiply and replenish the earth." A hearty welcome will be given by both husband and wife to the precious jewels which come into the home, providing the marital relations and other conditions are normal on the part of the parents.

It is indeed a sacred charge to take those young and tender human plants, rich with the possibilities of life, and become responsible for the moulding and developing of their mental, moral, and religious powers. Upon the parents rests the great responsibility of doing their utmost to so train and direct the lives of those jewels which have been divinely given into their charge, that they may grow up to be useful factors in the community, in society, and in the Church.

Fathers and mothers need to be a unit in the training of the children, and in bringing them up "in the nurture and admonition of the Lord" (Eph. 6:4). The faithful father will not shirk any of the responsibilities which are resting upon him in the rearing and training of the sons and daughters which are entrusted into his and the mother's care. He will not only provide the necessary food, clothing and other domestic needs of the family, but will make abundant provision for their mental, moral, and religious needs as well. Neither will he allow business and other secular duties to press him to the extent that he cannot spend sufficient time with his family to give them the assurance that they are his greatest earthly treasure. Nor will he consider his home a mere boarding house where he is expected to eat, sleep, and rest and spend the remainder of his time outside of the home in needless secular, social, and other pursuits; but his greatest delight will be to spend as much of his time as possible in home associations, taking advantage of every opportunity to faithfully perform his mission as a father toward his wife and children.

There are many, many fathers who are apparently sadly ignorant of their sacred parental responsibilities in the rearing and training of their offspring. They give infinitely more thought and care to the raising of live stock, increasing the farm products, extending their business affairs, or boosting certain political issues than they do in the more vital work of training their children. It is a fatal mistake on the part of any father to allow his business, social, or official affairs to crowd out his sacred home duties. Even the holding of some official position in the Church, the duties of which would require the father to neglect the proper teaching and training of his children, will not atone for any unfaithfulness in his home duties. Eli, the high priest and judge, may be cited to as an example of neglect in the training of his sons, "Because his sons made themselves vile, and he restrained them not" (I Sam. 3:13). The Lord punished him severely for his neglect.

The family is the primary, junior, and intermediate training school in which the pupils (the children) are taught and trained in the fundamental sciences which alone can make life worth living, both to themselves and others. The various compartments of the Home, or class rooms in which the family students are taught and trained for life's service, should be kept clean, tasteful, and inviting; even if void of ornamentation and decoration of art. It is seldom the case that a child will develop into a lovely, graceful, and congenial man or woman, with loveliness of character and purity of heart, if brought up in a home marred with the repulsive evidences and characteristics of filthiness, untidiness, slovenliness, vulgarity, harshness, and laxness in a general way.

All coarseness, bickering, wrangling, nagging, jangling and unkindness, need to be eliminated between father and mother lest the children, who are ready imitators, follow in their parents' steps. For the best interests of their posterity, parents should carefully guard their own lives, and train themselves to live together in peace, and manifest a true Christlike spirit in the family circle. A congenial and devoted spirit on the part of the parents has the effect of beautifying the home life, and bringing a delightful atmosphere within its walls, even though the rooms be plain and without any fancy touches. No home life can be more perfect than the life that is lived on the part of those who have established the Home.

Early training is much more effective in moulding the child's character than most parents are aware of. When the ground is moist and mellow the good seed should be sown, if it is to become truly fruitful. It seldom finds a lodging place in the soil after the same becomes dry and parched. The twig needs to be kept straight while it is yet young and tender, if the tree is to grow up straight and become symmetrical. It is impossible to bend and straighten it after it is full grown. When a stream is small its course can be easily changed, but not so when it becomes a river.

The mother wields the greater influence over her offspring. This being true, she needs divine guidance to faithfully perform her sacred duty of training her child for a life of usefulness, such as will prove a blessing to itself and others. It was faith unfeigned, coupled with early godly training, on the part of the mother and grandmother of Timothy, that resulted in making him a noble Christian worker and faithful Gospel message-bearer.

The mother may impart to the unborn child certain traits of character which will in after years have a tendency to develop either into noble Christian manhood or womanhood, or lead into channels of passion, vice, and sins most degrading. This being true, mothers should at all times be very careful to exercise a spirit of patience, kindness, and cheerfulness coupled with Christian fortitude; ever keeping the heart and mind pure, free from all passions and lusts which in any way might have an injurious effect upon the character of her offspring.

Observation reveals the sad fact that many who have through the grace of God been saved, and are walking in the way of Life, have had a continuous warfare and hard struggle against certain passions and evil propensities which have come to them by inheritance. Had the parents been conscious of what the effect of their indulgences would be upon their offspring, they undoubtedly would have exercised restraint and self-denial and thus counteracted the evil effects to a greater or less degree.

The mother's character, teaching, training, and example very frequently fixes the destiny of the child. From the Christian Home (which seldom exists without a Christian mother) flow forth the streams of love, faith, virtue, and purity to refresh the arid and parched deserts of a sinful world. With but few exceptions, the men who have been the greatest blessings to humanity, were men who had good Christian mothers. Dr. Cuyler says, "I doubt if I ever would have been drawn to the service of Christ Jesus, but for the faithfulness of that home preacher who rocked my cradle. At the starting point of nearly every minister's life there stands a Christian mother." The value of a noble, devoted Christian mother cannot be estimated. "Her price is far above rubies." Solomon presents a perfect picture of an ideal mother in Prov. 31:26-28, as follows: "She openeth her mouth with wisdom; and in her tongue is the law of kindness. She looketh well to the ways of her household, and eateth not the bread of idleness. Her children arise up, and call her blessed; her husband also, and he praiseth her."

A wicked mother is one of Satan's most successful agents to lead souls to ruin. It is said that Byron's mother was proud, ill-tempered and violent. From her he inherited the evil propensities which ended his short, passionate, profligate life. Nero's mother was a murderess. History records the terrible legacy left him by his mother. It is heart-rending to think of the awful physical, moral, and soul-destroying effects that have been wrought upon humanity through the influence of ungodly mothers.

While the mother has the greater influence over the child, nevertheless both parents are responsible to God for the moral and religious training of their children. Indeed, it is to fathers especially that the command is given to bring up children "in the nurture and admonition of the Lord." Christian fathers should not neglect the responsibilities which God has placed upon the head of the home. God's blessings or judgments are meted out to parents and their posterity, according as they have either discharged or neglected their duty. God's blessing rested upon Abraham and his posterity, because he was faithful in the training of those who were of his household. Note the eulogy that God paid to

Abraham: "For I know him, that he will command his children and his household after him, and they shall keep the way of the Lord, to do justice and judgment: that the Lord may bring upon Abraham that which he hath spoken of him" (Gen. 18:19). On the other hand, God pronounced judgment upon Eli and his house, because he failed to restrain his sons from committing sins of the most degrading nature. God said to Samuel, "The iniquity of Eli's house shall not be purged with sacrifice nor offering for ever" (I Sam. 3:14).

Great indeed are the possibilities and responsibilities of those who bear a relationship to other human beings so vital and sacred as that of the parent to the child. It is a relationship that results in momentous consequences. This being true, every parent should earnestly pray for the "abundance of grace" and wisdom in order to be enabled to faithfully discharge their sacred and solemn obligations in the Home.

The principles of truthfulness, honesty, gentleness, patience, and all other Christian virtues should be carefully taught and exemplified by the parents in the Home; yea, everything we wish our posterity to be in time and eternity should be taught and instilled into their minds and hearts while they are still members of the family circle in the Home. The divine command is to "train up a child in the way he **should go**," not as he **would go**, as some seem to understand Solomon to have said, judging from the course many parents pursue in dealing with the question of child-training.

A Tribute To Mother

Antoinette A. Lamoreaux pays the following touching tribute to a faithful, devoted mother:

"A great company had gathered in the auditorium for the evening service. There were men and women gray and bent, because the years had been long and full of care. There were young men and women with the morning glow upon their faces. Here and there sat a little child, and over all brooded the Sabbath hush.

Then softly in the silence began to steal the notes of a song—tenderly, yearningly, almost caressingly, it came:

> 'O mother, when I think of thee,
> 'Tis but a step to Calvary.'

"The silence deepened into a solemn stillness, as all the love and the longing, the joy and the sorrow, the disappointment and the achievement of the years poured themselves into the singer's voice. Again it came:

> 'O mother, when I think of thee,
> 'Tis but a step to Calvary,
> Thy gentle hand is on my brow,
> 'Tis leading me to Jesus now.'

"Then, as if the audience were but one great, hungry heart, hungry for mother, heads bowed, eyes

closed and song and singers were forgotten, the
sweetest face in all the world came back and with
that face a life. The long years gave up their store,
and a little child, a youth, a man was once again
with mother. Then, the heart made answer, the
common heart of the great, bowed audience made
answer to the song:

'Yes, mother, when I think of thee,
'Tis but a step to Calvary,'

"and thence to Calvary's God. And how easy it has
been to take that step, for mother was so like Him.
Her patience with our carelessness and willfulness
with our mistakes and foolish blunders helped us to
trust the mercy that endureth forever. Her spirit
which never thought of self, but always of another,
which counted sacrifice a privilege, if it enriched
the child she loved, had kinship with that Spirit
which gave the only begotten Son. Her confidence
in what we should sometime be, a confidence that
never faltered through all the wayward years, made
us understand in part how the heavenly Father
could await the perfected life of even His weakest
child.

"Her prayers interpreted to us the passion of
His intercession. Her smile gave us a glimpse of
the beauty of His face. Her readiness to hear any
childish confidence gave us added boldness to come
to Him, and her forgiveness—full, free and glad—
helped us to know how God forgives. It was her

touch in pain that told us of the Master's touch, it was her comfort in sorrow that gave meaning to the words, 'So will I comfort you.' It was her love, ministering, suffering, abiding, that moved us to reach our yearning hands toward the everlasting love of God.

"Yes, the song is true. Sing it once again and memory will join, reverently, lovingly, and gratefully.

> 'O mother, when I think of thee,
> 'Tis but a step to Calvary.'"

"The instructions received at a mother's knee, and the paternal lessons, together with the pious and sweet souvenirs of the fireside, are never effaced entirely from the soul."—**Lamennais**.

"Even He that died for us upon the cross, in the last hour, in the unutterable agony of death, was mindful of His mother, as if to teach us that this holy love should be our last worldly thought—the last point of earth from which the soul should take its flight to heaven."—**Longfellow**.

GEMS OF CHILD TRAINING

For the reader's careful and prayerful consideration, we herewith offer a number of brief suggestions along the line of child training, which we consider valuable gems worthy to be treasured up in memory's casket on the part of every parent:

*

Parents who wish to train up their children in the way

that they should go, must go in the way in which they would have their children go.

*

Parents should always stand together and be one in mind, purpose, and effort in the teaching and training of their children, if their work is to be blessed of God.

*

Parents should not fail to fulfil every promise made to their children. No promise should be made unless one is certain that the same can be fulfilled. If parents fail to keep their word with their children they will lose confidence **in** them and respect **for** them.

*

Children should not be given anything because they cry for it—absolutely nothing, great or small. They will soon form the habit of whining and screaming for everything they want, because they soon learn to know it means the granting of their wishes.

*

Do not allow children to become peevish or throw themselves on the ground or floor in a fit of screaming and kicking if their wishes are denied. The rod of correction, if rightly administered, is a sure cure for a habit of that kind.

*

Parents, do not punish your child for any misconduct while you are in an angry mood. To punish a child to simply give vent to your passion is injurious both to yourself and child. Be firm, yet discreet and gentle while administering correction, and your child will love, respect, and obey you.

*

Do not tease your children, neither make mention of their cuteness and witty remarks to others in their presence. It is a means of making them vain and conceited.

*

Children should be taught to be truthful, kind, courteous, tidy, economical, and, above all, to reverence God and all things holy. To be effective in the truest sense, these things must be taught by example as well as by precept.

*

The children should not be allowed to waste all their childhood days in play. They should be taught to work as soon as they are able, suiting the work to their size and age. The child needs to develop in physical strength, and should be early taught to become useful in the home and its surroundings.

*

Children should be well supplied with good moral and religious literature. Their characters will be moulded to a great extent by what they read. Anything of a trashy nature must not be allowed a place on the reading table, or in the home.

*

Look well after the associations of your children. If at all possible, never permit them to become intimately associated with any one who may be of a questionable character. Pure society tends to purity of life, which is of more value than treasures of gold.

*

Mothers, do not adorn your child's body with vanities you could not conscientiously put upon your own person. Those who do so are guilty of a twofold sin: (1) Teaching the child to become vain and proud. (2) Hypocrisy—pretending by their own appearance to be humble, when in reality they are proud at heart.

*

The girl in her teens, if she is physically well, should not be allowed to lie in bed while her mother prepares the breakfast and does the kitchen work. Such a course is injurious to both the mother and daughter, and in later years may prove a sad disappointment to some one in search of a good house-keeper and home-maker.

*

Mothers, do not get the popular though mistaken idea that in order to become an accomplished young lady, your daughter must have a college education, be an expert pianist, and efficient in doing all kinds of fancy work. These accomplishments do not bring real soul-refreshing sunshine into the home. An obedient, dutiful, helpful daughter who has added to her book learning the art of baking, cooking, sewing, and washing has the most necessary qualifications and acquirements to make the home an earthly paradise.

*

Parents should arrange to have all their children, if possible to do so, attend Sunday school and church services each Lord's day. They should be early taught to love and reverence the Lord's sanctuary.

*

Parents should never criticise the minister or any other Christian in the presence of their children. Rash and thoughtless criticism on the part of the parents has caused many a son and daughter to become irreligious and skeptical.

*

Daily family devotions, where prayer is offered, and the Scriptures are read and taught in a way that the children can understand its truths, is an essential means in leading them to accept its teachings and claim its life-giving promises.

OBEDIENT CHILDREN

Children, may you always obey
  Your father and mother so dear;
And seeking to please them alway,
  By bringing to them good cheer.

Count no sacrifice too great,
  To make for your kind mother;
Who cared for you early and late,
  And loved you as did no other.

Always be kind to your father,
  Who is greatly concerned for you.
He never counts it a bother,
  To help you be kind and true.

You owe your parents great respect,
  Whether you are a girl or boy;
Never your filial duty neglect,
  In bringing them refreshing joy.

Never fail in them to confide,
  When you have grave problems to solve;
Do not attempt from them to hide,
  That which your best interests involve.

As your kind parents older grow,
  Love's tribute to them always pay;
As pilgrims in this world below,
  They'll need your help along the way.

When the dear Father takes them home,
  To that world of sweet joy and bliss;
You'll not regret what you have done,
  To make them happy while in this.

CHAPTER VII

THE CHILDREN'S RELATION TO THEIR PARENTS

Children, obey your parents in all things; for this is well pleasing unto the Lord.—Col. 3:20.

Children, obey your parents in the Lord: for this is right. Honour thy father and mother, which is the first commandment with promise.—Eph. 6:1, 2.

The child while in its infancy is entirely helpless and absolutely dependent upon its parents, especially upon its mother for nourishment, care, and protection. As it grows in days and years it gradually becomes conscious of its relation to its parents, and if properly taught and trained the relationship becomes more and more intimate on the part of the child, and more useful and helpful to the parents. The child is dependent upon its parents for food, clothing, protection, instruction and training; the child in turn owes to its parents its love, respect, esteem, honor, and faithful obedience.

Children are, as David says, "An heritage of the Lord," hence have their being or existence primarily through the providence of God, and secondarily through earthly parentage. Hence their relation to both God and their parents is such that they owe to both their loving obedience and faithful submission in all things.

Those scriptural requirements given to children

should inculcate perfect fidelity in the discharge of filial duties toward parents. Those children who are kind, respectful, and obedient to their parents are pursuing the course which will mean great blessings to themselves, their parents, the Church, and the world.

As a father, and one who is greatly interested in the children and young people of this and future generations, the writer is impressed to say with Solomon, "Come, ye children, hearken unto me, I will teach you the fear of the Lord." I earnestly entreat you as children, whatever be your age, circumstances, and environments in this world, ever to submissively, readily, and cheerfully hearken to and obey the counsels and commands of your parents in all things that are consistent and right, being constrained through love towards them and Christ to lovingly submit to their authority and thus do that which "is well pleasing to the Lord."

According to both human and divine laws, obedience and respect are the just dues which children owe their parents at all times. These filial obligations apply to the children of every nation, kindred tribe, and tongue. "Honor thy father and mother" is the first commandment of the second table of the moral law given from Mt. Sinai, and it is the first commandment that is followed with a definite promise: "That it may be well with thee, and that thou mayest live long on the earth." Such a wonderful promise should be an incentive to constrain every child, boy or girl, young man or maiden, and those who are older in years, to conduct themselves toward their parents in the most affectionate, respectful, submissive, obedient, and helpful manner possible, that through the blessing of God (because of their obedient attitude toward their parents) their lives may be prolonged and be happy.

The writer was intimately acquainted with an aged saint whom the Lord permitted to live three years beyond the century mark. As she neared the close of her earthly pilgrimage of five-score years and three, she was asked by those who called to visit her, whether she knew why her life has been spared so many, many years. She replied, "It is because the Lord has promised me long life, for He said, 'Honor thy father and thy mother, that thy days may be long upon the land which the Lord thy God giveth thee,' and I never knowingly disobeyed my father and mother, hence He has kept His promise in giving me a life of many years."

It would be well if every son and daughter would follow the example of Jesus as a child, a bo and a young man, who was reared in the home of His mother and foster father at Nazareth, and "was subject unto them" and "increased in wisdom and stature, and in favor with God and man" (Lu. 2: 51, 52). Though Jesus was the Son of God, His glory being veiled with a body "made in the likenc .

of sinful flesh," He became subject, not only to His heavenly Father's will, but also subject (for a score and a half years) to those who were divinely appointed to rear him, and supply His needs while growing up to manhood and preparing Himself for His soul-saving mission in this world. We see in that lowly home in Nazareth a vivid picture of a holy Child: a boy and young man who constantly manifested toward His mother and foster father the most perfect submission, obedience, and helpfulness, working with His hands to help supply their home needs. We are confident that His obedience was not by constraint, but prompted by the spirit of true love and cheerfulness. No one will question as to whether He did His part faithfully in making the Nazareth home an ideal domicile. At the age of thirty years, after having faithfully fulfilled His mission in His Nazareth home, this loving, obedient son of Mary left the parental affiliations and as the Son of God went forth to fulfil His divine mission in bringing the Gospel of salvation to a lost world, and after three years of sacrificial service in healing, helping, and saving fallen humanity He paid the penalty of the world's sin on Calvary. While in great agony on the cross He did not forget His loving mother, but made provision for her temporal needs by delegating John the beloved disciple to take her to His own home and take care of her. Wonderful indeed was the devotion and thoughtfulness manifested on the part of Jesus our loving Savior toward his mother! All children should earnestly seek to "walk in His steps."

Implicit, unquestioning, and cheerful obedience to the will of the parents is the highest duty of children, and is the best preparation for future allegiance to the divine laws which were given by God the Father, and the Lord Jesus Christ our Savior, for the government of their lives.

Because of the depravity of human nature, children are naturally inclined to become self-willed, disobedient, stubborn, rebellious. These tendencies may to a great extent be counteracted by careful prayerful, vigilant training.

From its infancy the child should be taught instant and unhesitating obedience. If the child manifests a disposition to be self-willed or stubborn, it is very essential that its stubbornness be conquered and the child be firmly but kindly made to render absolute obedience, or submission. To teach or inform the intellect of the child will necessarily take time, and must be accomplished by degrees as the child can grasp and retain; but the conquering of the child's stubborn inclination must be attended to at once, while yet in the bud, if the best results are to be realized. By neglecting timely correction along this line the child will naturally be inclined to acquire an obstinate disposition which is seldom if ever conquered in after years. It is not only a serious neglect, but it is absolutely wrong for parents to allow their children to form habits or traits of character which they know must afterwards be broken. or overcome both for their own good and the good of others. The mother of John Wesley said, "Self is the root of all sin and misery, so, whatever cherishes this in children, insures their after wretchedness and irreligion; whatever checks and mortifies it, promotes their future happiness and piety." The parent that studies to subdue the spirit of selfishness in the child becomes a coworker with God in preparing it for a life of usefulness. The child that is taught to submit to the will of the parents will the more readily submit to the will and Word of God when it is grown.

If children would consider how tenderly their parents cared for them when they were helpless infants; how they kindly fed, clothed, and provided for all their needs during the years they could not provide for themselves; how lovingly and diligently they taught them "line upon line, and precept upon precept;" how earnestly they prayed that their feet should be directed in the narrow way, and how vigilantly they watched for their development in all that is noble and true, they certainly would at all times manifest loving respect, esteem and obedience to their parents in every possible way. It is a sad fact, that children as a rule are slow to comprehend how greatly their parents love them. Too often they fail to realize the depth of father's and mother's love and sacrificial service which had been manifested toward them as children, until their parents are called hence by the angel of death, or until they are blessed with children of their own.

Faithful children will honor their father and mother, not only while their parents live, but as long as they themselves live. Children who honor, love, and obey their Christian parents usually reap a blessed harvest in their own posterity. Paul said: "Whatsoever a man soweth, that shall he also reap." This is a sentence which is very manifestly verified, both in the matter of training children and in the children's attitude and conduct toward their parents.

Those who are blessed with Christian parents and are still under their charge as sons and daughters, should greatly appreciate such a privilege and constantly manifest sincere gratitude to both father and mother, and thus endeavor to compensate them for their parental love, tender care, deep concern, devoted attention and self-denying service rendered them in their domestic relations.

As a son or daughter, never allow yourself to (in any way) disrespect your parents, or be in the least ashamed of them, even though they may not be what you consider ideal in every respect. They may lack in intellectual training, or seem somewhat old-fashioned in appearance and method of doing things, or what you would (if inclined to be fastidious) consider more or less out of date; nevertheless if your heart beats true to your parents, and they have been true to you in their sacred trust, you will readily see in them such qualifications and traits of character, as are infinitely the most essential in giving you the needed training for a life of usefulness, and the highest and noblest conception of an ideal life.

Rich blessings will rest upon those who give heed to the following scriptural injunctions: "My son, hear the instruction of thy father, and forsake not the law of thy mother, for they shall be an ornament of grace unto thy head, and chains about thy neck" (Prov. 1:8, 9).

The father's hands may have become calloused, his face may be wrinkled, his steps becoming slower and slower, and as a result he may have lost some of his physical attraction in your eyes as his child; but it is well for you to consider that those hands became hardened by incessant toil on his part to provide for your various needs. Those wrinkles in his face may have been caused on account of his deep concern for your best welfare, and those dilatory steps may be the result of his hurried efforts to smooth life's pathway for you as his son or daughter. Be sure to remember the conflicts and struggles your father endured for you, and despise not his bent form, his calloused hands, his care-worn face, nor his hoary locks, but treasure the same as unmistakable tokens of his deep love for you, and of hardships endured, sacrifices made, and great things accomplished for your best interests, both for time and eternity.

The most devoted of all human affection is that of a mother's love for her children. This being true, every child, whether son or daughter, should at all times manifest the most devoted and affectionate attitude toward the mother who gave them birth, and who spent many days in teaching them to look, think, walk, talk and sing; and later on to be useful in lending a helping hand in performing little tasks in and about the home, which meant much to both mother and children.

Honor and respect should never be withheld on the part of children from the one who above all others prayed, toiled, endured, and spent many sleepless hours in kindly caring for her priceless jewels, when they were passing through seasons of sickness, suffering, trials, temptations and disappointments. Indeed, great should be the honor bestowed upon the mother who so tenderly watched over her children and instructed and directed them as they were developing into manhood and womanhood, thus preparing them to wisely and bravely face the perplexing experiences in life, also moulding their characters for real usefulness in the Church.

Children should ever seek to do their part well in honoring and obeying their parents, in order to express their appreciation for all the love and parental care bestowed upon them in their infancy and youth, also during their manhood and womanhood days. Expressions of gratitude and appreciation should never wane on the part of the children toward their parents that they may be a crown of honor to them in old age. The love, care, self-denial, and helpfulness so bountifully lavished upon children on the part of the parents should not only be constantly remembered by children thus favored, but lovingly reciprocated in every way possible by bringing sunshine into their lives until they are called hence by the hand of death.

FILIAL GEMS

"Hear, O my son, and receive my sayings; and the years of thy life shall be many."—**Solomon.**

*

"My son, forget not my law; but let thine heart keep my commandments: For length of days, and long life, and peace, shall they add to thee."—**Solomon.**

*

Self-denial, manifested on the part of children in seeking to please their parents, is one of the most positive evidences of true filial love.

*

Children should show their love toward their parents by confiding in them in the most intimate way, making them the recipients of all their confidences.

*

"The children that speak every thought, every hope, every ambition, every plan, every pleasure in the ear of their parents will live safely."—**Miller.**

*

If love, respect, and honor for parents has its seat in the heart, there is little need of rigid rules and discipline in the Home, because true affection is the constraining power which prompts loving obedience.

A dutiful son is an honor to his father and mother, a valuable asset to the community in which he lives, a helpful factor in society, and will prove a blessing to the world.

*

A faithful, devoted, obedient daughter is of infinitely greater value in the Home than the finest architecture, decorations, and drapery that can be used in beautifying it.

*

As children be thoughtful, cheerful, courteous, and patient in your domestic affiliations, ever manifesting the spirit of love, and true submission toward your parents; and you shall be not only happy, but become a real blessing both to your parents and others.

*

The Christian Home is the school where the children are taught the vital principles of character moulding; where their hearts are enthused with pure motives and desires, their minds developed and turned heavenward, and their souls made to hunger and thirst after righteousness.

*

"Let all children remember, if ever they are weary of laboring for their parents, that Christ labored for His; if impatient of their commands, that Christ cheerfully obeyed; if reluctant to provide for their parents, that Christ forgot Himself and provided for His mother amid the agonies of the crucifixion. The affectionate language of this divine example to every child is, "Go thou and do likewise."

*

"Honor thy parents; those who gave thee birth, and watched in tenderness thine earliest days, and trained thee up in youth, and loved in all. Honor, obey, and love them; it shall fill their souls with holy joy, and shall bring down God's richest blessing on thee; and in days to come thy children, if they're given, shall honor thee and fill thy life with peace."—**Edwards.**

*

"Never forget where your mother lost her freshness and youthful beauty—it was in self-denying toil and suffering for your sake. Those wrinkles in her face, those deep carelines in her cheeks, that weary look in her eye—she wears all these marks now where once there was fresh beauty because she has forgotten herself these long years in loving devotion to you. These scars of time and toil and pain are the seals of her care for you."—**Miller.**

SERVANTS AND MASTERS

Servants

Servants, may each one of you,
  To your masters be always true,
Obeying them in everything
  That has in it the Gospel ring.

Obey the froward and the good,
  And may it be well understood
That God's commands you must uphold,
  As by the Scriptures you are told.

Seek to please them from day to day,
  Being faithful in every way,
And if you always faithful be,
  Your Lord will say, "Well done" to thee.

Masters

"Masters, give unto your servants"
  That which is just, lawful and right;
Expecting of them true service
  When present, and when out of sight.

Exact no more than what is just,
  And do not their confidence shake.
Reward them, when true to their trust,
  And you will not make a mistake.

May your relationship ever be
  Patterned after the "Golden Rule,"
Because Christ your Master is He
  Who has taught you thus, in His school.

CHAPTER VIII

THE RELATION BETWEEN MASTERS AND SERVANTS

> Servants, obey in all things your masters according to the flesh; not with eye service, as menpleasers; but in singleness of heart, fearing God; and whatsoever ye do, do it heartily, as to the Lord, and not unto men.—Col. 3:22, 23.
>
> And, ye masters, do the same things unto them, forbearing threatening: knowing that your Master also is in heaven; neither is there respect of persons with Him.—Eph. 6:9.

Paul defines very vividly the nature of the relationship that should at all times exist between servants and their masters. To enlarge upon what he has written may to some seem superfluous. We consider it very essential to both servants and masters to have a true comprehension of the relation they sustain to each other as Christians, hence we shall endeavor to set forth in this chapter at least a few helpful thoughts bearing upon the relationship referred to above.

Servants are required by divine law to render faithful Christian service to those who are their "masters according to the flesh;" that is, to those in whose employ they are and to whom they owe obedience in all things which do not conflict with the principles of righteousness. Faithful servants will promptly and cheerfully obey their masters, providing they are not required to do things which are displeasing to their Master which is in heaven.

The true Christian servant is ever desirous to please his master, for in so doing he knows that he is honoring Christ and promoting His cause. He will not only be subject to the "good and gentle, but also to the froward," the master that is inclined to be peevish, petulant, or perverse. The submissive servant realizes with Peter that it "is thankworthy, if a man for conscience' sake endure grief," suffering wrongfully" (I Pet. 2:18, 19).

The service rendered must not be a constrained external service, or that which is simply superficial intended to attract or catch the eye of the master or some one else, but a service prompted by the sincere motives of the heart; rendered in kindness, cheerfulness, and readiness; having regard to God and a sincere desire to please Him, who is the rewarder of all faithful service regardless as to whether the individual is bond or free.

Every servant, whether bond or hired, young or old, male or female, should diligently seek to obey every consistent command or request of master or mistress, recognizing the fact that they are divinely required to render faithful service to their masters, whether the same are believers or not. All true Christian servants will endeavor to execute faithfully the trusts committed to them, and obey every command without hesitancy so far as is consistent with the teachings of Christ. The service will not be of a slavish nature and done reluctantly and grudgingly, but with a willing and ready mind, from a sense of loving duty to the Lord Jesus Christ, in obedience to His command and with a view to His glory, and not from any selfish or mercenary spirit, which aims only at pleasing self or attract the eyes of men.

There are those who consider it very humiliating and even debasing to be somebody's servant. There is no occasion for any one to consider it a position that is in the least dishonorable to be a servant, providing the one who acts in that capacity is faithful in discharge of his or her duty as a servant, and if the nature of the service is sinless. To be a servant is to minister to the needs of others, and make sacrifices for their good. All true Christians are servants whether they are in the employ of some one else or not. It is encouraging to know that the pathway that leads to true greatness is the pathway of service. Our blessed Lord "made himself of no reputation, and took upon him the form of a servant.... wherefore God also hath highly exalted him, and given him a name which is above every name" (Phil. 2:7, 9). After our Lord and Savior had emptied Himself and relinquished the glory He had with His Father, and came to this world of sin and sorrow to become a sacrificial servant in redeeming and lifting up fallen humanity through the shedding of His blood, He was highly exalted by the Father as Mediator and Head over all things pertaining to His Church.

Those who aspire to sanctified greatness in life need to obey the loving Master's teaching and His lowly example as recorded in Matt. 20:27, 28 which reads as follows: "Whosoever will be chief among you" (that is, of real spiritual worth) "let him be your servant" (most active in ministering to the needs of others), "even as the Son of man came not to be ministered unto, but to minister, and to give his life a ransom for many." How wonderful this beautiful picture portrays Christ's loving, self-sacrificing, redemptive service! Our Savior also said, "I came not to do mine own will, but the will of him that sent me." This ideal relationship which existed between our heavenly Father and His only begotten Son should be the relationship sustained between Christian servants and their masters; that is, perfect submission to the will of the one whom we are called to serve.

Masters are to be governed by the same supreme regard to God's Word, which actuates the lives of faithful servants. They should at all times manifest the same, kind, charitable, and cheerful readiness to please God in their conduct toward their servants, as the servants are required to manifest toward them. The relation between servants and their masters is a relationship that should be governed at all times by the Golden Rule—servants doing for their masters what they in turn would wish their masters to do to them, and, if the tables were turned, masters treating their servants as they would wish to be treated if called to take the servants' place. If this rule is applied by both servants and masters, a relationship will exist between them which will bind them so closely together that when it becomes necessary to separate, the thought of separation will bring real sorrow to both parties. "As the eyes of servants look unto the hand of their masters, so our eyes wait upon the Lord our God."

If servants should either willfully or unintentionally fail to render faithful service, masters should manifest a real Christian spirit toward them; instead of threatening and treating them harshly, they should seek to win their obedience and good will by manifesting a spirit of love and forbearance toward them. Masters, your servants are your brethren, at least by creation if not by regeneration; children of the same heavenly Father; redeemed by the same loving Savior, and as a master you will finally stand with them before the same impartial judge. You will not receive special favor in the day of judgment because you were masters, and your servants will not be less favored because they were servants. As a master your more elevated position increases your responsibilities, and if you fail to manifest a congenial spirit toward your servants, your condemnation will be increased.

Paul in addressing the believers at Colosse said: "Masters, give unto your servants that which is just and equal:" that is, which rightfully, according to the law of God, belongs to them, and that which fairness and honesty require. "Knowing that ye also have a Master in heaven" to whom they as believing masters owe faithful service and who requires them to render to their servants all things which equitably and honestly belong to them, and to manifest toward them the spirit which they as masters would wish Christ to manifest toward them.

We greatly regret that in certain homes, even among those who profess to be Christians, domestic servants are considered too far beneath the dignity of the master and mistress of the home, to be allowed to enjoy equal privileges with the children and visitors to eat together at the same table in the dining room; and when visitors are being entertained in the home, the servants are expected to be careful not to intrude by coming into the room where the company is, unless called upon, either by the master or mistress of the home to do so. In certain sections of the country it would be considered a mark of great disrespect for a colored servant to dine with the family whom he or she is serving. It is indeed sad to know that laws of etiquette are more carefully observed on the part of masters and mistresses in their relation to servants than are the laws which are divinely given to govern the relation between masters and servants.

CO-OPERATIVE GEMS

Obedience, is the passport giving the servant admission to his master.'s approval, and to his own success in his calling as a servant.

*

Servants should make it an ironclad rule to render absolute obedience to their masters, providing they are not asked to violate any principle of righteousness.

*

"He that is called in the Lord, being a servant, is the Lord's freeman; likewise also he that is called, being free, is Christ's servant."—**Paul.**

*

"The disciple is not above his master, nor the servant above his Lord. It is enough for the disciple that he be as his master, and the servant as his Lord."—**Jesus.**

*

"Exhort servants to be obedient unto their own masters, and to please them well in all things; not answering again."—**Paul.**

*

"No servant can serve two masters; for either he will hate the one and love the other; or else he will hold to the one, and despise the other."—**Jesus.**

*

It is well for masters or mistresses to close their eyes to the imperfections and shortcomings of their servants, and keep them wide open to their good traits of character and faithful endeavors of service.

*

The master's mission towards his servant is not only to give commands and pay just wages, but also to exercise prudence, patience, and Christian courtesy at all times.

*

Masters, in commanding servants remember to do so in a respectful, reasonable, and brotherly way; ever keeping in mind the Golden Rule, making a faithful effort to apply its principles at all times.

*

"We must truly serve those whom we appear to command; we must bear with their imperfections, correct them with gentleness and patience, and lead them into the way to heaven."—**Fuller.**

*

"It is not only paying wages and giving commands that constitutes a master of a family; but prudence, equal behavior, with a readiness to protect and cherish them, is what entitles man to that character in their very hearts and sentiments."—**Steele.**

*

"Expect not more from servants than is just; reward them well if they observe their trust; nor with them pride or cruelty invade, since God and nature them our brothers made."—**Denham.**

*

"Servants, be obedient to your masters according to the flesh, with fear and trembling, in singleness of your heart, as unto Christ."—**Paul.**

*

"Exhort servants to be obedient unto their own masters, and to please them well in all things; not answering again; not purloining, but showing all good fidelity; that they may adorn the doctrine of God our Savior in all things."—**Paul.**

*

The master who is filled with the spirit of Christ will ever manifest an attitude of love, kindness, and tolerance toward those who are his servants, even though their service is not ideal in every respect.

*

The relation between masters and servants should be reciprocal at all times—masters manifesting wisdom, prudence, and appreciation toward those who serve them; and servants in turn rendering submission and faithful service to their masters, as **unto Christ.**

HOME PROBLEMS

There are many serious problems,
  Looming up for people to solve;
Some apply to business only,
  Others which their souls involve;

Problems which affect the family,
  Leading to either weal or woe;
It is well to solve them promptly,
  And in the safest way we know.

Whether it's a social problem,
  Applying to the children's need,
Or whether a life vocation,
  Both should be given careful heed.

Or whether it is education,
  Training faculties of the mind;
The problem should be well considered,
  That the right solution we may find.

If it is the marriage question,
  That may be giving much concern;
There should be prompt action taken,
  To solve this problem in its turn.

If the problems we'd wisely solve,
  We'll need the wisdom from above;
To direct in their solution,
  For the best welfare of those we love.

CHAPTER IX

PROBLEMS TO BE SOLVED IN THE HOME

Hear, ye children, the instruction of a father, and attend to know understanding. For I give you good doctrine, forsake ye not my law....My son, attend to my words; incline thine ear unto my sayings: let them not depart from thine eyes; keep them in the midst of thine heart.—Prov. 4:1, 2, 20, 21.

King Solomon was desirous to give both his and other children such instructions as would tend to beautify their characters, enhance their best interests, promote them to positions of honor, multiply their blessings, and crown their heads with ornaments of grace and glory, if the same were carefully observed. Thus they would be enabled to walk safely in the paths of righteousness and acquire wisdom to satisfactorily solve life's problems.

It requires more than human wisdom to solve the many difficult and momentous problems which come up in the Home. Divine wisdom, or the wisdom which comes from above (which "is first pure, then peaceable, gentle, and easy to be entreated, full of mercy and good fruits, without partiality, and without hypocrisy,") is the kind needed on the part of parents to enable them to wisely solve their domestic problems. Problems which are exceedingly grave frequently arise in the family circle, and the weal or woe which is likely to come to the child in after years depends largely upon how these problems are solved before the son or daughter goes out from under the parents' guardianship.

Problems which affect the state are solved by the state legislature. Those which affect the nation are discussed and solved by our national representatives at the nation's capitol. Those affecting the welfare of the Christian Church are discussed and (at least to a certain extent) solved in our Church conferences. But the problems which affect the welfare of the world are solved in the institution called Home.

The proper solving of the vital problems which arise in the homes of our land, is the foundation stone upon which is built everything that is noble, good, and true, found in society, in business, in professional life, in government, and in religion.

The Word of God, if diligently studied and rightly understood, will supply Christian parents with the much needed equipment to satisfactorily solve every problem affecting the moral, social, and religious life of each individual member of the family.

The problem of training the child properly is one that must be solved by the parents. The child's nature and temperament must be carefully studied and such methods of training applied as will be most effective in making the child what God intended it

should be. Methods that will most judiciously re-
press the first manifestations of rebellion and protest
against parental authority, and all such tendencies
as are likely to develop into hurtful habits and evil
conduct. Methods by which all that is good, pure,
noble, and true may be impressed on the child's
mind and instilled into its heart. To successfully
accomplish this all important end, the parents need
to be in constant touch with God, looking to Him
for divine guidance in moulding the child's character for a life of real usefulness.

The problem of the child's education is one that
needs to be judiciously solved by the parents. No
parents who know the worth of mental training and
development will question whether their child, or
children, shall be educated, but to what extent? a-
long what lines? by what means? and in what institutions of learning? These are usually the questions which puzzle the minds of the parents.

An education does not necessarily mean the
completion of a college, seminary, or university
course. In the truest sense, education means more
than to be proficient in mathematics, history, geog-
raphy, botany, astronomy, zoology, physiology, and
other sciences; something more than having mas-
tered the dead languages, yea, much more than can
be acquired by the most laborious effort of the human intellect. It is the drawing out, the developing, the strengthening and training for usefulness in

life, every faculty of the body, mind, and spirit.

The problem of the child's education should by all means be solved to the best interests of the child, and its influence for good in the world, carefully guarding against any educational methods or influences, as would have a damaging effect on the child's spiritual life.

The moral training of the child must also be carefully looked after. The problem as to how the son or daughter may be safely guided through the age of puberty is one that needs very thoughtful consideration in order to be able to judiciously solve that delicate problem. Parents cannot afford to neglect their sacred duty in giving their boys and girls the proper information, instructions, and warning at this critical period in directing their young lives into channels of virtue. Neglect along this line on the part of the parents may result in the most debasing and degrading vices, which have the effect of sadly corrupting and blasting the lives and characters of those who are led to practice such sinful indulgences, and often untold misery is brought upon their posterity.

The matter of the children's associations should be directed by the parents with constant vigilance. If the child's character is to remain unsullied by evil influences, it must be restricted from associating with children who are vile, profane, and disobedient, and later shown the imminent danger of becoming intimately associated with those of questionable character, or loose in morals. To permit such associations to continue usually means ruination to the son or daughter, and brings reproach upon the parents. The child is a treasure infinitely more valuable than any earthly treasure, hence needs to be vigilantly guarded lest the enemy come in unawares in the form of some human agency and rob its soul of innocency, purity, and true happiness.

To provide the children and young people with the right kind of literature is also a problem of no little importance. With the present abundant supply of good moral and religious literature which is to be had at a price within reach of all, there is no excuse for not having the home well supplied with such periodicals and books which if read can be used to great advantage. A good instructive book is a friend "that sticketh closer than a brother." Brothers and sisters frequently leave home, at least for a short time, but the good book as a silent friend, remains in the home and is ready to talk at all times to every member of the family circle.

The problem of choosing one's vocation, profession, or calling, is also one that needs thoughtful consideration on the part of the parents and all concerned. The wise, thoughtful, prayerful direction of the parents should be prudently exercised in helping the son or daughter in making a decision so important. The child's natural inclinations, tendencies, likes, dislikes, and preferences should be carefully studied, and its energies directed toward the vocation or calling for which he or she is naturally adapted, and at which success would most likely be realized—providing it is an honorable vocation or calling, and one that will prove helpful to all concerned.

Another momentous problem is that of choosing life companions—the joining of hands and hearts in the marriage relation. Young people cannot be too careful as well as prayerful, in the selecting of life companions. The marriage relation brings with it the most solemn obligations, and momentous consequences. Therefore sons and daughters who are brought face to face with this weighty problem, should not fail to take their parents into their confidence and consult them as to the advisability of taking such an important step in plighting vows with one of the opposite sex—a step that will either lead to greater happiness, successes, and rich blessings both in time and eternity, or to a life of sorrow, slavery, and perpetual misery. Parents by their wise counsel along this line may be instrumental in bringing perpetual blessings upon their offspring.

Kind reader, if you should contemplate entering the marriage relation, as you love your soul and its eternal welfare and the best welfare of others who through the providence of God may be added to the family circle, as you regard your peace and future happiness, as you value the commands of God and His loving favor, never form such a relationship with any one, however amiable, however moral, however endowed with the gifts of fortune and nature, who is not a true Christian. But only with such an one who will gladly share your joys and sorrows, your successes and reverses, your victories and defeats, and your varied conjugal experiences, as you journey together through life in the Master's service.

The problem that is greater than any other is that of church affiliation, which needs to be more carefully and prayerfully considered and acted upon than that of the child's education, vocation or calling, social relations, or marriage. After children have come to the years of accountability, it is the paramount mission of Christian parents to put forth every divinely ordained method to lead them to accept Christ as their personal Savior, help them to develop in all the Christian virtues and principles, and thru earnest prayer and wise counsel direct their course of procedure in being identified with the Church and its activities. It is of vital importance that both parents and children belong to the same body of believers, which is a means of binding them together with a twofold bond of love and fellowship which is very sacred and encouraging to all connected with the family group.

A home cannot be ideal in the truest sense unless parents and children are of one mind, one in heart, one in the faith, one in purpose, and one in Christian service. In counseling together as parents and children, relative to church affiliations, it should always be in the spirit of prayer and perfect submission to the teachings and principles of God's Word. The church that measures up the nearest to the true Gospel standard is the Christian organization with which the entire family should be identified.

Uniting with the Church is a very essential step to be taken by every Christian believer whether young or old. The nature of the step is so vital, solemn, and serious that no one can afford to take it without giving the matter very prayerful consideration. It brings the believer into a sacred and active relationship with his Lord and Master. In becoming allied with Christ's body (the Church) we become coworkers with Him; not thinking merely as to what the Church may do for us, but more especially what we may be able to do for the Church. It is indeed a sacred privilege to be a member of the true Christian Church, and any one who is so highly honored as to be a member of the body of Christ should diligently seek to be worthy of the sacred relationship which he sustains to his blessed Lord and Master.

PROVERBIAL GEMS

The Product of Solomon's Pen

"A word fitly spoken is like apples of gold in pictures of silver."

*

"A wise son heareth his father's instruction."

*

"Hear instruction, and be wise, and refuse it not."

*

"Hearken unto me now therefore, O ye children, and attend to the words of my mouth."

*

"My son, hear the instructions of thy father, and forsake not the law of thy mother."

*

"A wise son maketh a glad father; but a foolish son is the heaviness of his mother."

*

"A foolish son is the calamity of his father."

*

"A foolish son is a grief to his father, and bitterness to her that bare him."

*

"My son, give me thine heart, and let thine eyes observe my ways."

*

"My son, if thine heart be wise, my heart will rejoice, even mine."

*

"Hear, O my son, and receive my sayings; and the years of thy life shall be many."

*

"Wisdom is the principal thing; therefore get wisdom; and with all thy getting get understanding."

*

"My son, if sinners entice thee, consent thou not; walk not thou in the way with them; refrain thy foot from their path."

*

"Whoso keepeth the law is a wise son; but he that is a companion of riotous men shameth his father."

"He that gathereth in summer is a wise son; but he that sleepeth in harvest is a son that causeth shame."

*

"Hear counsel, and receive instruction, that thou mayest be .wise in thy latter end."

ADVISORY GEMS

"Children are not so much to be taught as to be trained. To teach a child is to give him ideas; to train is to enable him to reduce those ideas to practice."—**W. H. Beecher.**

*

"Education commences at the mother's knee, and every word spoken in the hearing of little children tends toward the forming of character.—Let parents always bear this in mind."—**H. Ballon.**

*

It is well to remember that children can take in but little teaching each day. They are like bottles with a narrow neck, which may hold considerable but can take in but little at a time.

*

Parents need to diligently teach and instil into the minds and hearts of their posterity the principles of morality, which are manifested in purity, honesty, and truthfulness, all of which are products of the Christian religion.

*

"We should be as careful of the books that we read as of the company we keep. The dead very often have more power than the living."—**Edwards.**

*

It is not so much what people eat, but what they digest, that gives them strength. It is not the money they make, but what they save, that makes them wealthy. It is not how much they read, but what they remember, that makes them well posted. There are three things that should prompt us to be diligent readers: (1) to become informed as to the existing conditions in this present world; (2) to become qualified to faithfully perform our daily tasks; (3) to bring our minds, hearts, and souls into a proper relation to our heavenly Father.

A mother was printing on a blackboard a text for her little daughter. The text was: "Christ Jesus came into the world to save sinners." Just as she had finished it the child entered the room and began to spell out the words. Presently she exclaimed, "Oh, Mamma, you have left out Jesus!" True enough, she had left out that blessed name in writing out the sentence. It is indeed sad if any one should take the momentous step in entering the marriage relation and leave out Jesus. To establish a home without the presence and guidance of the loving Master means the lack of the paramount factor in making the wedded life truly happy, and the home ideal in the truest sense.

FAMILY DEVOTIONS

Seek in the early morning hour,
  Before the breakfast call is heard,
To gather a sacred flower,
  From the Bible, God's blessed Word.

Read prayerfully with thought and care,
  Also with pleasure and delight;
After reading, kneel in prayer,
  In the morning, also at night.

As parents you should not falter,
  Or neglect your sacred duty;
In erecting a family altar,
  If your home you'd crown with beauty.

Listen to the voice of Jesus,
  As He lovingly speaks to you;
Knowing it your Master pleases,
  When to Him you are always true.

The lessons are truly precious,
  Which we learn from His holy Word.
The promises are most gracious,
  Which from its pages may be heard.

God's living Word will life impart,
  To those who feed upon the same.
And thus the mind, the soul and heart,
  Will be filled with love's sacred flame.

CHAPTER X

THE MORAL AND RELIGIOUS ATMOSPHERE OF THE HOME

> Thou shalt teach them diligently unto thy children, and shalt talk of them when thou sittest in thine house, and when thou walkest by the way, and when thou liest down, and when thou risest up.—Deut. 6:7.
>
> My voice shalt thou hear in the morning, O Lord, in the morning will I direct my prayer unto thee.—Psa. 5:3.

The Lord gave specific instructions to the fathers in Israel as to how they were to instruct, teach, train, and rear their children. The moral and religious training of them is a divine requirement of all generations of the Christian Church, hence is binding upon every Christian parent in this present age, but alas, how many, even of those who claim to be loyal Christians, come far short of fulfilling their solemn obligations in the all important work of teaching and training their children as the Lord hath commanded!

The physical, intellectual, moral, and religious development of the child should have the parent's careful and prayerful attention. Many parents make the sad mistake in doing a one-sided work in the training of the child. Being influenced by the trend of the times, special attention is given to the physical, or intellectual development of the child at the expense of the more essential, that of the moral and religious training, which is infinitely more valuable to any young man or woman than are physical drills, mathematics, the sciences, and the dead languages. The more mental power one has, the more capacity for evil, unless coupled with moral and religious restraint, backed by a true Christian character. The education of the intellect must be accompanied by a thorough education of the heart, or there may be an energy aroused within the child that will mean a blasting influence in its life later on. In our homes great opportunities present themselves in the way of building up true manly and womanly character, which may mean much in strengthening the Christian Church and bettering world conditions.

Fathers and mothers, it is for you to decide whether from your home shall go forth young men and women who shall be a credit to your name or not; whether a blessing to the world or not; whether a glory to God and His cause or not.

The principles of purity, truthfulness, honesty, gentleness, patience, courtesy, and all other Christian virtues and graces should be taught and exemplified by the parents in the Home; yea, everything we wish our posterity to be in time and eternity should be taught and instilled into their minds and hearts while they are under the parental roof. Children are close observers, and very much inclined to imitate the words and actions of their parents, whether they be good or bad. This being true, parents should be very careful as to their example. To teach by precept is divinely required of parents, and if the same is to become effective for good in the lives of the children, all such teaching needs to be constantly exemplified on the part of the parents. Heavenly benedictions are sure to rest on homes and families of this kind.

There is nothing that can be established in the Home that is of greater importance and is as essential in the development of true Christian character in the family and community as daily reverent, informative family worship. Such worship should not only include the reading of the Scriptures but also a clear, practical explanation of the passage or passages read, so that the children and all present in the family may have a true conception of the teachings of God's Word, which is given to direct both parents and children in their relation to one another, and to others outside of the domestic circle; also to God the Father and the Lord Jesus Christ as their Savior. In homes where the Bible is read daily in the presence of the children, and its lessons simply and prayerfully explained and taught, the effect for good cannot be comprehended with the finite mind. It was thus that God instructed His ancient people to do. They were to teach the truths of His Word diligently to their children when they sat in the house and when they walked by the way, when they rose up and when they lay down. This was God's plan for rearing and instructing the rising generations in that age, and continues to be—not simply teaching the children a scriptural lesson now and then when it may seem most convenient to do so, but the incessant, uninterrupted daily mission of teaching and instilling into the hearts and minds of the children the sacred messages and principles of God's Word. Such teachings, if given in the spirit of love and prayer, will unconsciously make a lasting impression upon the mind and heart of the child, which will help mould its character for real usefulness in this world, and perfect happiness in the world to come.

As each day the family listens to the voice of God as He speaks to them through His life giving Word, they should be constrained through love to come before Him in the spirit of true devotion and gratitude and have a heart to heart talk with Him through prayer, in which should be expressed the spirit of reverence, adoration, praise, thanksgiving and submission, followed by humble confession and an earnest appeal for grace and strength to meet the day's trials, temptations, and perplexities, and to faithfully perform the duties of the day. The reading of God's Word and prayer are the two essential means of grace. In the reading of God's Word He speaks to us in a plain, loving manner, revealing to us His precious commands and promises, which by grace divine are to be hidden within our hearts. Bunyan said that "prayer is a sincere, sensible, affectionate pouring out of the soul to God, through Christ, in the strength and assistance of the Spirit, for such things as God has promised."

As the physical body needs to be nourished with wholesome food each day for its daily tasks, even so the soul needs to feed upon the "sincere milk of the Word" at the beginning of each new day, in order to be enabled to faithfully perform its arduous daily duties. Children do not alone receive a lasting benefit from such a daily service, but parents themselves receive from it a most helpful stimulus for their own spiritual life; thus being enabled to faithfully fight life's battles, and be an influence for good not only in the family circle, but in a general way among those with whom they come in touch from day to day.

David said to his Lord, "My voice shalt thou hear in the morning, O Lord; in the morning will I direct my prayer unto thee." This should be the motto in every Christian home, the essence of which should be fulfilled and verified every day in the week from year to year until the transition is made from earth to glory.

Every Christian should spend some time each day in private devotions, where the soul can pour out its longings and appeals to God, with none to molest, no one to see and hear except the loving Father, Son, and Holy Spirit. But these secret devotions cannot take the place of the open service around the family altar where every member of the family may join in the songs, reading of the Word, and prayer. These family devotions should be conducted at least once each day. The morning hours are preferable to any other time of the day, because as a rule the children are wide awake at this time, and their minds are receptive of the lessons taught. Some one has said, "In the morning, prayer is the key that opens to us the treasures of God's mercies and blessings; in the evening, it is the key that shuts us up under His protection and safeguard."

The first act of the soul in early morning should be to feed at the table of the Lord which is so sumptuously spread in His Word, and to take a draught of the water of life at the fountain of heavenly grace. It will greatly strengthen the soul and sweeten the life for the day. A few moments with our loving Master at that calm and tranquil hour of the day are of greater value in smoothing life's pathway, and imparting peace to the soul, than are all earthly treasures. Each day should be opened with prayer, continued in prayer, and closed with prayer and praise.

Christian parents cannot afford to neglect to establish family worship in the Home, and when established they cannot afford to allow any work, business, or the cares of life to crowd out the sacred service. It is the hour in which the soul puts on its armor and prepares itself for the faithful performance of its daily duties. Dr. Miller very fittingly says, "Bowing in prayer together in the morning strengthens all the household for life's active duties. Wisdom is sought and obtained for the decisions and plans of the day. Guidance is asked and received. Help is drawn down from the throne of God. The children go out under sheltering wings and are safe in danger, guarded by angels and kept by Christ Himself."

No iron-clad rules should be laid down as to how the family devotions must be conducted. We believe that for best results various methods should be used. To prevent monotony it is well to at least occasionally change the order of the service. Reading of the Word, prayer, and singing should be the three chief elements of the service. Such selections of Scripture should be read, from which practical lessons can be drawn, that will tend to be helpful to both the children and all who are present in the family circle at the time. The Daily Readings which are given in connection with the Sunday school lessons are usually appropriate, and not too lengthy. When comments are made on the lesson read, the same should not be of great length, but to the point, in order to be the most helpful and effective in building up Christian character.

The father (if a Christian) should have charge of the devotions, but it is not advisable for him to do all the reading and praying, unless there are no other members of the family who are able to assist in the service. It is well to have each member of the family take turns in reading the Scripture lesson, or each one be supplied with a Bible and each one read a verse in turn. The children and other members of the family who are Christians should at least occasionally be called upon to lead in audible prayer. Such home training will not only mean rich blessings to the children in the Home, but will greatly facilitate the best interests of the Sunday school and other public religious services, because both parents and children are thus more or less prepared to participate in a co-operative service in the study of God's Word.

It is very essential that the family worship be conducted in a way, that the same may be of special interest to the younger members of the family, as well as to those who are older in years. In some instances the service is conducted in a way that it becomes irksome and wearisome to at least some extent. Long chapters are read, and sometimes of a chronological nature, and often in a lifeless and drone-like manner. The prayer is usually of a stereotyped nature day after day. The petitions are frequently the same and of the most general kind, touching all classes and conditions of men except the little group which are kneeling around the family altar, and embracing humanity's needs in general rather than the needs of the immediate family. So often there is nothing in the service that draws the attention of the children toward the loving heavenly Father and gracious Savior who are, each day, so abundantly supplying both their temporal and spiritual needs. There can be no justifiable reason for so conducting the religious services that the same will become dull and irksome to any member of the family group. The family worship should be of such a nature that it would mean a season of real soul refreshment to the entire family, its refreshing features eagerly anticipated from day to day, and its memories prove to be the most hallowed of all home recollections.

The impressions made upon the children in homes where family worship is conducted daily, are such that when young men and women they go out from the parental home to fight life's battles for themselves they are to a great degree safeguarded against the influences of sin, because of the sacred influences brought to bear upon them around the family altar. There are no earthly treasures which parents can bequeath to their children that are of such great value to their posterity, both for time and eternity, as the inestimable blessings received through the influences of a godly home.

Dr. Miller very strikingly portrays the worth of

the sacred influences of a godly home, as follows:
"If parents give money to their children, they may
lose it in some of life's vicissitudes. If they bequeath to them a home of splendor, they may be
driven out of it. If they pass down to them as a
heritage only an honored name, they may sully it.
But if they fill their hearts with the holy influences
and memories of a happy Christian home, no calamity, no great sorrow, no power of evil, no earthly
loss, can ever rob them of their sacred possessions.
The home songs will sing themselves out again in
the years of toilsome duty. The home teachings will
knit themselves into a fiber of character, rich in its
manly and womanly beauty, and invulnerable as a
coat of mail. The home prayers will bind the soul
with gold chains fast to the promises of God. Then,
as the years go on and the old home of earth is
broken up, it only moves from behind, as it were,
and goes on before, where it draws the soul toward
the better life."

Eternity alone will reveal the problems that
have been solved, the difficulties that have been overcome, the burdens that have been lifted, the victories
that have been won, the days that have been brightened, the peace that has been enjoyed, the souls that
have been made happy, and the blessings that have
been realized on the part of those who have been
reared in homes that have been enriched with sacred
devotions.

Fathers and mothers, do you desire to teach and train your children for the Master's service in this world, and the unspeakable joys of the eternal world? If so, do not neglect to gather them together at least once a day in the study of God's Word, and in earnest prayer commit them to the loving care, guidance, and protection of Him who "shall supply all your need according to his riches in glory by Christ Jesus."

DEVOTIONAL GEMS

"Evening, and morning, and at noon, will I pray, and cry aloud; and He shall hear me."—**David.**

*

"Ask and ye shall receive, seek and ye shall find, knock and it shall be opened unto you."—**Jesus.**

*

Prayer is the key that unlocks God's store-house of grace, and prepares the heart to receive its priceless treasures.

*

Each day should be hallowed by the early morning devotions, which if properly conducted will furnish the needed strength for the day's duties.

*

Every Christian home should be filled with the halo of God's presence. This can only be realized by praising Him daily for His infinite goodness, and imploring His love and sustaining grace in the spirit of true reverence and devotion.

*

They that wait daily upon the Lord in the spirit of sacred devotion, rise higher and higher into the realms of grace, and through the eye of faith become possessors of God's precious promises, which are treasures worth infinitely more than all earthly treasures of silver and gold.

Private devotions coupled with the open service around the family altar, are the refreshing seasons which quicken the soul and prepare the individual for the faithful performance of life's duties.

*

A prayerless home is minus of true heavenly blessings. The dispenser of those blessings is denied the privilege of being a guest in such a home. This being true, the family is not abiding "under the shadow of the wings of the Almighty;" hence cannot be assured of His protecting care in the truest sense of the divine promises.

*

Angels encamp around the true Christian Home; even David had this assurance when he said: "The angel of the Lord encampeth round about them that fear Him, and delivereth them." It is indeed encouraging to know that God's protecting wings are over the homes where His children dwell, and the interior of each Christian Home is sweetened and made joyful by the divine presence.

*

"Till I come, give attendance to reading....Meditate upon these things; give thyself wholly to them; that thy profiting may appear to all." "Study to show thyself approved unto God, a workman that needeth not to be ashamed, rightly dividing the word of truth."—**Paul.**

*

"The best and sweetest flowers in paradise, God gives to His people when they are on their knees in the closet. Prayer, if not the very gate of heaven, is the key to let us into its holiness and joys."—**Brooks.**

*

"All the duties of religion are eminently solemn and venerable in the eyes of children. But none will so strongly prove the sincerity of the parent; none so powerfully awaken the reverence of the child; none so happily recommend the instruction he receives, as family devotions, particularly those in which petitions for the children occupy a distinguished place."—**Dwight.**

*

"It is of utmost importance to season the passion of the young with devotion, which seldom dies in the mind that has received an early tincture of it. Though it may seem extinguished for a while by the cares of the world, the heats of youth, or the allurements of vice, it generally breaks out and discovers itself again as soon as discretion, consideration, age, or misfortunes have brought the man to himself. The fire may be covered and overlaid but cannot be entirely quenched and smothered."—**Addison.**

A PARENTAL CHARGE

As parents be ye ever true,
To the charge committed to you
In teaching and training your children dear.
Seek their lives to carefully mould,
Before they leave the parental fold,
That they may enjoy a useful career.

Shield them from all manner of sin,
And all that is to it akin,
By placing safeguards within the home.
Thus protecting their lives from harm,
And all such things that cause alarm,
That they're not left in darkness to roam.

There are numerous destructive foes
Which bring to children awful woes,
When admitted into the domestic life.
Home happiness will take its flight,
When those vile monsters come in sight,
Because they gender wrath, hatred and strife.

Teach by precept and example,
Which methods are truly ample,
To mould and train the Child's heart and mind.
If your work is to stand God's test,
You will need to do your very best,
Helping your child its way to Heaven find.

CHAPTER XI

THINGS TO BE DISCOURAGED, AND ELIMINATED FROM THE HOME

> My son hear the instruction of thy father, and forsake not the law of thy mother....Enter not into the path of the wicked, and go not in the way of evil men....Keep thy heart with all diligence; for out of it are the issues of life.—Prov. 1:8; 4:14, 23.

Solomon was divinely inspired to give children of all generations wise counsel and valuable instruction, in order that their lives might be so governed and directed that their characters would be moulded in accordance to God's plan and approval. He stands as a representative of every true Christian father and mother, whose paramount aim should be to so instruct their children that they may be trained for real useful service in life.

The instruction given needs to be both of a positive and negative nature. The negative is just as necessary and as essential in moulding character as is the positive. By a careful study of Proverbs (chapters 3 and 4) it will be clearly revealed to the reader that great blessings follow in the wake of acquiring true wisdom (the beginning of which is "the fear of God") and meekly submitting to parental instruction, both of which are positive require-

ments of God's Word. It is also clearly revealed
that great blessings are realized in obeying the negative commands, by not entering "into the path of
the wicked," and not going "in the way of evil men."

It is absolutely necessary on the part of every
son and daughter, regardless of their environments,
to keep their hearts with all diligence, if they are
desirous to keep their characters unsullied from the
ravages of sin. The life of the individual is governed
by the desires and inclinations of the heart; hence
if the heart is allowed to harbor evil thoughts, im-
pure motives, and sinful desires, the life becomes
corrupt and antagonistic to all that is good, and
pure, and holy. This fact is verified by the statement made by our Lord and Master when He said:
"A good man out of the good treasure of his heart
bringeth forth that which is good; and an evil man
out of the evil treasure of his heart bringeth forth
that which is evil" (Lu. 6:45). It is very necessary
that parents, and all others who are entrusted with
the sacred and solemn obligations of training children and young people, to faithfully guard their
young lives from the ravages of sin, not only teaching them the principles of righteousness but diligently warning them of the danger of being associated with those who are classed among the wicked.

Everything that has a tendency to lead the rising generation into channels of indifference, worldliness, selfishness, impurity, and sinfulness of any

kind should be vigilantly guarded against, and denied any foot-hold whatever in the family circle. In fact, everything that tends to cultivate looseness in adhering to the principles of righteousness, anything that has a corrupting influence upon the character of any one in the family group, yea, anything that would tend to pollute the Christian atmosphere of the Home, should be eliminated from the Home by those who are in charge of its sacred realm.

Many parents, especially mothers, are very careful to make their homes inviting by keeping the same free from dust, filth, and general disorder. The real tidy home-makers are to be commended. It is however of infinitely greater importance that the homes and families be kept free from the dust and filth of sin, and everything that has a tendency to lead the rising generation into sin and its corrupting and destructive influences.

The Home is the garden where the buds develop into fragrant blossoms and delicious fruit; hence it is very important that the garden (Home) be kept free from weeds, and such insects as have a tendency to destroy the fragrant, nourishing and luscious products of the garden. Influences that are very slight may serve to blight the opening buds, and the valuable crop be completely ruined. This being true, every Christian parent should put forth every possible effort to keep the children (the tender plants of the home garden) free from the destructive influences of the weeds of evil, and the insects of sin.

Human nature is naturally inclined to do that which is evil. Traits of evil are very noticeable in the lives of children, and if such tendencies are not forestalled and counteracted by thoughtful, careful, prayerful action and godly influence on the part of parents the result may mean serious calamity to both themselves and their posterity later on. The child's character is being moulded and formed as noiselessly as the falling of snow-flakes. We fail to see the unfolding of the bud as we stand and look at it, but when on the morrow we look for the tiny bud we behold with surprise the fragrant flower. Even so it is indeed difficult for us to recognize each day the growth of the child's character; but as the days pass into weeks, months, and years we notice very clearly the forces that are gathering in the child's mind, heart, and life which manifest themselves in characteristics that will either blossom into beauty and fragrance of real life or manifest the evidences of blight, baseness, and repulsiveness of character.

Precept and **example** need to be coupled together on the part of the parents in seeking to discourage and counteract the things that are useless, trivial, and questionable in and about the Home, and in eliminating the things which are harmful, corrupting, and sinful. As a rule children are more easily influenced by example than by precept. A child may be told repeatedly that dishonesty is sinful; but if the child should detect dishonesty in father or mother, brother or sister, he or she will be most likely to imitate the example. A good example on the part of parents is a mighty force in inculcating the principles of truth, honesty, purity, and righteousness in the hearts and lives of the sons and daughters of this and all generations.

The lewd, vulgar, profane, and desperately ungodly persons who will be used as Satan's agents during the next generation, are now the little innocent children in the arms of mothers in various parts of this sinful world, children who are now being influenced by sinful home agencies.

Every family is exposed to innumerable dangers through the weaknesses of the flesh, the encroachments of the world, and the seductions of our terrible adversary, the devil. Enemies are seeking to desecrate the sanctity of the Home and rob it of its sacred treasures. The agencies of modernism, infidelity, disloyalty, and unchastity are given inroad into many so-called Christian homes. Many social influences of a questionable nature tend to disintegrate the home life, robbing it of its sanctity and breaking down the sacred barriers which had been erected to preserve the purity of the institution called Home. Nothing but the cross of Christ manifested and exemplified in a life of self-denial will be effective in saving our children for Christ and His Church.

We shall call attention to a number of destructive agencies that need to be carefully guarded against, and denied admittance and toleration within the sacred precincts of the Christian home. The agencies of evil are diversified in nature, but all are destructive to godliness. They assail the purity and sanctity of the Home from without and within, making assaults on the mind, heart, and soul of the individual. The home atmosphere, comforts, purity, and religion are seriously affected by the many present day evils which are everywhere so prevalent.

Anger and **Grouchiness**—are two of the peace-destroying agencies in many homes. They are twin evils which should be carefully avoided. To be angry about trifles is silly and childish, to get into a rage and become furious is brutish, and to continue in a state of anger is to become demon-like. Such cruel monsters should be kept isolated from the family circle every day in the year. If perchance they should, in an unguarded moment, gain access to the Home and disturb any member of the family, they should be immediately muzzled and cast out by the armor of God, which is so definitely described in Eph. 6:11-18.

Harsh and **Unkind Words**—are the audible manifestations of anger, which serve as fuel to intensify the flames so destructive to the "fruit of the Spirit," "love, joy, peace, longsuffering, gentleness," etc. All such hurtful and evil tendencies as anger, wrath,

malice, hatred, impatience, harshness, rudeness, etc.,
need to be counteracted and by God's grace eliminated from the Home. This alone can be done through
the spirit of love, kindness, forbearance, and longsuffering coupled with watchfulness and prevailing
prayer.

Parents and children should all earnestly endeavor to "let patience have her perfect work" in
every phase of their domestic life, and thus scale
the highway leading to Christian perfection.

Selfishness and **Waywardness.**—These two mon-
ster twins have caused more grief, distress, disappointment, and calamity in the Home than any other evils, because they are universally manifested in
human nature. Selfishness is the mother of the
largest family of sinners upon the face of the earth.
Selfishness is in reality the root of all sin, and the
source of all natural and moral evils. It causes the
individual to have a perverted view of his or her
own life, and the life and character of others. It is
also blind to one's best interests both in this life and
in the life beyond. The great "I" which manifests
itself so ostensibly in the lives of the multitudes in
all ranks of society, is the very center of sin, S-I-N.

These things are manifest in the disposition of
children as well as in those of maturer years, hence
it should be the great aim and purpose on the part
of parents to inculcate the spirit of self-sacrifice and
submission in the hearts and lives of their children.

Self is the greatest idol in the universe, and its worshipers are innumerable, represented in every kindred, tribe, and nation. All who are self-centered have really made an idol of self, and are not only desirous that others worship them, but are actually worshiping said idol (I-doll) themselves. There are no carnal agencies more destructive to spirituality than selfishness. It was selfishness, or the promptings of self-interest, that led mother Eve to partake of the forbidden fruit, which meant the awful downfall of the human race and the transmission to humanity, of this deceptive characteristic.

Self-love is an affection that is very unprofitable, leaving the soul in a condition of sad disappointment because it is void of everything that is of a true satisfying nature.

Parents should be diligent in shielding their offspring from the ravages of selfishness, which if not curbed will lead them to become self-centered, wayward, and rebellious, all of which are characteristics foreign to the Christian virtues mentioned in Col. 3:12-14. Children are "diamonds in the rough" that need to be polished with the divinely ordered methods of influence, teaching, and discipline.

Pride, Vanity, and **Conceit**—are triplets, and very much alike in appearance and character. Pride is the fountain source of both vanity and conceit, and is the impelling power within the heart and mind, which constrains the individual to make a vain and empty display of self in the way of gaudy dress, frivolous adornment, and haughty poise, and furthermore it is manifested in overestimating one's own abilities and talents, thus giving evidence of being puffed up either because of rank, beauty, accomplishments, or high social standing, all of which are the product and evidences of pride.

There are multitudes that rob their souls of true love and happiness, to feed their pride and vanity. It is very evident that pride, vanity, and conceit are bitter enemies to the Cross religion, and because of their artificial beauty and fascinating appearance these soul-beguiling agencies are blasting and destroying infinitely more of the human race, than are the evils of a more depraved nature. These subtle, fascinating sins are not only making inroads into millions of socalled Christian homes, but into the most of the churches and, sad to say, these sinful parasites are sapping the spiritual life out of many of the churches.

Vanity and conceit coupled with Fashion compose the roots, trunk, branches, leaves, blossoms, and fruit of the tree called Pride. Solomon said: "Pride goeth before destruction, and an haughty spirit before a fall." Of all human characteristics, pride is the one that most seldom obtains its end, or the thing sought for, hence the most disappointing. It aims at honor and reputation, but as a rule reaps contempt and derision.

Vanity and conceit engender affectation. They are the parents of mock modesty. They feed upon the trivial things of life, with the purpose of making a display and attracting attention to self, which so manifestly poses as the great "I." These seductive enemies of modesty and humility, are no respecter of persons; they seek to get into the good graces of both saint and sinner. This being true every parent should carefully guard against these all-pervading soul destroying agencies.

The goddess of Fashion has undoubtedly more worshipers in this present age than any other object of worship. A certain author has said: "No other god or goddess has ever had more zealous devotees than fashion, or a more absurd and humiliating ritual, or mortifying and cruel penances. Her laws are like the Medes and Persians, they must be implicitly obeyed but, unlike them, change as certainly as the moon. They are rarely founded on reason, usually violate common sense, sometimes common decency and uniformly common comfort. Fashion rules the world, and a most tyrannical mistress she is, compelling to submit to the most inconvenient things imaginable for her sake." This soul-destroying goddess needs to be barred from every Christian heart, life, and home.

Some one has said that the votary of Fashion "consults the fashion-plate oftener than her Bible. She visits the dry goods shop and milliner oftener than the Church. She speaks of Fashion oftener than of virtue, and follows it closer than she does her Savior. She can see squalid misery and low-bred vice without a blush or a twinge of the heart; but a plume out of fashion, or a table set in old style, would shock her into a hysteric fit. Her example! What is it but a breath of poison to the young?"

Christian parents who are interested in the best welfare of their posterity and the Church should constantly keep the portals of the Home closed a-gainst those ostentatious evils, and use every possi-ble means to eliminate the same from the family circle.

Untruthfulness, Profanity, Vulgarity, and **Fault-finding**—are a quartette of evils, that proceed from a depraved heart and give expression through the instrumentality of the tongue which, James says, "setteth on fire the course of nature, and it is set on fire of hell" (Jas. 3:6). The tongue is simply the index or indicator of the condition of the heart, as Jesus says: "Out of the abundance of the heart the mouth speaketh." Jesus further says: "By thy words thou shalt be justified, and by thy words thou shalt be condemned" (Matt. 12:34, 37).

The Word of God specifically forbids jesting, vulgarity, boasting, flattery, slander, back-biting, ly-ing, cursing, profanity, and blasphemy. An unbri-dled tongue gives positive evidence of a depraved and sinful heart, is used of Satan to stir up hatred and strife, and brings reproach upon others, even upon those who are blameless in life and character.

James says that the tongue "is an unruly evil, full of deadly poison." This being true, how necessary that parents have their heart purified and their tongues tamed by the grace of God, in order to be able to give their children the proper teaching in the proper use of their tongues. Peter says, "He that will love life, and see good days, let him refrain his tongue from evil, and his lips that they speak no guile" (I Pet. 3:10).

Slovenliness, Idleness, and **Negligence**—are very unfavorable characteristics, which frequently manifest themselves in the lives and conduct of children. If these traits of character are not counteracted while in their youthful years, they will become fixed habits in life, and will mean serious results later on.

Luxury and **Extravagance** — are evils which manifest themselves in seeking to please the senses with hurtful indulgences, satisfying the appetite with luscious eats, and in the unnecessary expenditure of money. These popular evils need to be carefully guarded against on the part of parents, if their work is to count for the best interests of their children.

Filthy and **Sinful Habits**—also need to be carefully guarded against on the part of the parents, and if any such habits have already entered the Home and enslaved any member of the family, every justifiable effort should be put forth to eliminate the habits. The tobacco habit is undoubtedly the most popular of all the filthy habits that has enslaved humanity. The use of the narcotic weed— either in chewing, smoking, or snuffing it—is not only a filthy habit but it is injurious to the body and cannot in any way be used to the benefit of the individual, nor to the glory of God. Hence the same should be laid aside immediately lest the effect upon your life and influence will prove serious both to yourself and others.

I entreat you, dear Christian parents, to faithfully discharge your sacred duty in shielding your posterity from the ravages of the many social and moral evils so prevalent in this day and age, that they may become polished jewels for the Master's kingdom.

NEGATIVE APPEALS TO PARENTS

Since the Home as an institution has been divinely founded, it should be the paramount aim of those who have plighted vows, and are made one in the sacred bonds of matrimony, to so order their domestic life and family affairs, that the Home will not only be properly established but governed according to the Heavenly Father's plan. In order to accomplish this great work, it is absolutely necessary to be diligent in keeping the doors of Home closed against everything that is of a questionable or sinful nature, whether in thought, word, or action.

*

As parents, do not fail to look daily to the Lord for His guidance and sustaining grace, to enable you to make your home as nearly ideal as possible, every day in the year—not only by embellishing its various apartments with things that tend to beautify, purify, and enrich its atmosphere and every phase of the home life, but by eliminating from its sacred sphere everything that has a tendency to mar, degrade, pollute, pervert, and dissipate those who are members of the family circle.

*

Do not fail to teach both by precept and example, and diligently shield your posterity from the influences of sin, if you wish your work to be effective in moulding their characters and lives, that they may shine as jewels for the Master, both in this world and in the world to come.

*

Mothers, do not fail to put forth every effort to make your homes inviting by keeping the same free from everything that is of a filthy, unsanitary, disorderly, unsavory, disagreeable, and obnoxious nature.

*

If interested in the best welfare of your children, do not neglect your duty as parents, to so teach and train them that they may be safe-guarded from becoming indolent, extravagant, untruthful, dishonest, conceited, selfish, and unchaste.

*

As parents, do your utmost to keep the atmosphere of your home pure, sweet, and refreshing by keeping it free from questionable conversation, unkind words, harsh expressions, slanderous statements, false accusations, severe criticisms, vulgar utterances, and profanity.

*

We entreat all parents to carefully safeguard their children from attending places of worldly amusements—such as picture shows, theatres, dances, carnivals, and all questionable entertainments. These worldly pleasure resorts and entertaining functions are Satan's most effective agencies to counteract the work and effects of Christianity.

*

As Christian parents, be careful not to give your youthful sons and daughters the privilege to spend their spare moments and evenings away from home, at places and in company which are unknown to you. The teen age of your children should be carefully guarded because of the subtle temptations and destructive influences which are so prevalent on every hand.

Fathers, if you are interested in the best welfare of your sons, do not give them license while in their teens, to use your automobile in a promiscuous way, either at night or on the Lord's Day. The use of autos on the part of pleasure-seeking youth, in what is called "Joy-riding," is leading many souls into the awful sin of immorality.

*

That which children and young people read is largely instrumental in moulding their characters. Hence great care needs to be exercised in keeping all books, periodicals, papers, etc., of a fictitious, trashy, exciting, deceptive, corrupting, and demoralizing nature, constantly eliminated from the Home.

HOME DECORATIONS

The Ideal Christian Home will be,
  A restful paradise below;
A place where love flows full and free,
  And hallowed joys at all times flow.

A place of restfulness and peace,
  Where kindness makes its constant calls;
A place where friendships never cease,
  And all is peace within its walls.

A fortress built upon the rocks,
  Of honesty, virtue, and truth;
A refuge free from cruel knocks,
  That might mean harm to noble youth.

A school of morals and of grace,
  Where youthful lives are trained with care,
It is indeed a sacred place,
  Where constant joys, each one may share.

Cheerfulness should brighten the home,
  And contentment its rooms adorn;
Devotion should be its sacred dome,
  To shelter all from sin and storm.

Friendship and joy, and perfect peace,
  Should in the home be made to grow;
They'll tend Home's blessings to increase,
  And make it a Heaven below.

The Bible, the most sacred Book,
  Should be daily and carefully read;
By thus taking an upward look,
  The soul will be divinely led.

CHAPTER XII

THINGS TO BE ENCOURAGED, AND ESTABLISHED IN THE HOME

> Whatsoever things are true, whatsoever things are honest, whatsoever things are just, whatsoever things are pure, whatsoever things are lovely, whatsoever things are of good report; if there be any virtue, and if there be any praise, think on these things.—Phil. 4:8.

The foregoing admonition was given by Paul to the Philippian believers. He refers to a number of Christian characteristics which they as Christians were urged to think upon, and make practical in their lives. These very vital principles of righteousness and godly virtues need to be not only thought about but diligent efforts should be put forth to both teach and exemplify them in the Home from day to day.

If the Home is to be made ideal, and one of God's flower gardens from which there shall go forth sweet perfume having a purifying effect upon the unwholesome atmosphere of society and the world, it will be necessary that those in charge take diligent heed to Paul's admonition, instilling into the minds and hearts of the rising generation the things that are in harmony with true Gospel principles.

Every father and mother should not only diligently teach but also practice and cling to the things that are effective in moulding nobility of character, things that promote sincerity and truthfulness, things that are decent and in order—in the way of dress, conversation and deportment—as is becoming to Christian men and women; things that are just and due to our fellow men, also to God the Father and the Lord Jesus Christ as a Savior; things that relate to chastity in body, mind, and heart, also in purity of speech and behavior; things that render a person acceptable to God and agreeable to man. Each member of the family—including parents, children, and servants—should earnestly and prayerfully study the nature, advantages, and necessity of those godly qualities and carefully and constantly put them into practice.

Home should be made the sacred shelter and refuge of our lives, whether we are rich or poor. All things that are needed to furnish and adorn the Home with happiness, peace, and true domestic fellowship are mentioned by the inspired apostle in Phil. 4:8.

Parents should seek to make Home so truly home-like that when the weary, tempted son or daughter who may be traveling the rugged pathway of life after being severed from home ties, he or she will gladly, because of home attractions, turn homeward again to receive help, comfort, and encouragement. The Home should be made a real haven of rest and encouragement to every member of the family.

Home should be made a paradise of real heavenly beauty and a refreshing fountain in the wilderness of life, where each member of the family circle may drink of water (to quench their soul thirst) that is unmixed with any of the world's bitter ingredients—water composed of spirit reviving elements, imparting health and strength to all the members of the household. Those who drink of the world's vain pleasures simply become partakers of artificial excitement for the present, and those who entertain worldly ambitions in their minds become deluded with passing golden dreams which soon vanish. It is only true Christian love, and domestic peace and joy, that can produce a life that is truly happy and blessed.

In this concluding chapter we shall call attention to a number of things that need to be encouraged, taught, and exemplified in the Home.

Love.—The loving Master said to His disciples (which includes every Christian): "These things I command you, that ye love one another" (Jno. 15: 17). Love is the constraining power that prompts and lavishes its various expressions of affection upon the object it admires, or worships. It is impossible for the human mind to fathom the depth, scale the height, and comprehend the greatness of love.

True domestic love, coupled with divine love, has a preserving and purifying power. As a certain writer has said: "It sends an ever swelling stream of life through the household. It binds hearts into one bundle of life. It shields them from temptation. It takes the sting from disappointments and sorrow. It breathes music into the voice. It lightens the footsteps. It gives worth and beauty to the commonest office. It surrounds Home with an atmosphere of moral health. It gives power to effort and wings to progress." It is love that happifies memory and makes home beautiful. It is of such a refining and elevating character that it expels from our hearts and lives the things that are base and degrading, and leads us to think and do things that change our clay tendencies into aspirations and deeds like unto gold.

Love is the great illuminating sun, the unifying bond, the joy-creating virtue, and the soul-inspiring grace in every ideal Christian Home. Parents should enthrone love as the crowning diadem in the Home, and never give it occasion to take wings and fly away.

Joy.—Jesus said, "These things have I spoken unto you, that my joy might remain in you, and that your joy might be full." The joy that is enduring and satisfying, is the joy that is within the soul and is divinely given to the Christian believer. Earthly joys are fleeting. They are gathered as flowers the fragrance of which is enjoyed but for a short season, then the flower withereth and the fragrance vanisheth, and the same becomes disappointing and offensive. But true joys within the soul are abiding, a means of inspiration and refreshment even in times of trial and affliction. True Christian joy brings cheer and comfort to the heart three hundred and sixty-five da s in the year, regardless as to whether the sun shines or not. Such joys are a means of real refreshing to the soul, and bring to us a foretaste of the eternal joys of heaven.

Peace.—Our blessed Lord said to His disciples: "Peace I leave with you, my peace I give unto you." The inestimable gift of peace was given to Christ's disciples as a means of calming the heart, while engaged in their warfare against sin, and to be constantly enjoyed in the sheltered recesses of the Home. Every father and mother should diligently seek to adorn their home with true peace, which is a wonderful factor in calming the troubled waters, soothing the ruffled hearts and minds, and bringing about a state of tranquility when storms of various kinds seem to threaten the family domicile.

Honesty.—"Providing for honest things, not only in the sight of the Lord, but also in the sight of all men" (Paul). The sin of dishonesty is very prevalent in the world—in fact, in almost every phase of life's affairs. It has made astounding inroad into political, social, business, and even religious affairs. Conditions will continue to grow worse and worse along the line of dishonesty, unless parents make it an iron-clad rule to close the doors of the Home against every inclination toward dishonesty, and on the other hand diligently seek to instill into the minds and hearts of their sons and daughters the principles of honesty in every phase of their lives. This can be best accomplished by making the "Golden Rule" the practical rule of conduct in the Home.

Truthfulness.—Jesus said, "Let your communication be, Yea, yea; Nay, nay; for whatsoever is more than these, cometh of evil" (Matt. 5:37). Regardless of whether the statements are of a positive or negative nature, the same need to be an expression of truthfulness, if they are to be void of evil. God is the author of truth, and the devil is the author and father of lies. Truthfulness should be expressed both by words and acts on the part of every member of the family, and at all times and under all conditions.

This ennobling trait of character is a part of the divine equipment which Paul mentions in Eph. 6:14. Those who lack this part of the Christian armor will not be able to overcome the evil forces which assail all those who are running the Christian race. Truthfulness should not only be encouraged, but permanently instituted and practiced in every Home.

Economy and Industry.—These two very essential Home servants are the agencies which ward off the wolf of poverty and keep the hateful sluggard from entering the doors of the Home. They provide the domestic abode with the needed comforts—such as food, clothing, home furnishings, and other necessary things. Every outlet of useless expenditure, and inclination to idleness should be discouraged and carefully guarded against with constant vigilance, that the seeds of extravagance and slothfulness are not permitted to germinate and grow within the family circle.

Children should be early taught to save their pennies, nickles, and dimes, and be made to realize that their own future comforts and prosperity, will depend largely upon their saving and making the proper use of the small amounts of money which may come into their possession. The principle of economy, if properly taught, and instilled into youthful minds, will mean great blessings to themselves and others in after years.

Industry has a similar effect upon the future life of the child. A strict regard to economy and industry does not only keep one's own larder well provided with the needed supplies for physical support and comfort, but enables one to lend a helping hand in relieving the needs of others.

Patience and Kindness.—These are twin sisters, and the most congenial companions in the Home.

The social atmosphere is anything but inviting where these sisters are absent. Peter exhorts believers in general to add "to patience godliness, and to godliness brotherly kindness." Thus we are clearly shown that patience and kindness are to be inseparably united with godliness, which is expressed in piety and devotion.

Because of the weakness and depravity of human nature, and the varied traits of character coupled with egoism, it is of paramount importance that each member of the family exercise patience and forbearance in their domestic relations.

Patience is expressed in calmness and serenity in all the trying experiences of life, and it is the means of fostering unity in the family, in the community, and in the Church. It causes one to be cheerful in adversity, unmoved by reproach, and manifests the spirit of forgiveness when wronged by any one. A certain author has said: "Patience is the guardian of faith, strengthens the spirit, sweetens the temper, stifles anger, extinguishes envy, subdues pride; she bridles the tongue, restrains the hand, tramples upon temptations, consummates martyrdom."

One of the luscious fruits of patience is kindness, which is composed of expressions of words and actions prompted by love. Like the little drops of rain that moisten the earth and clothe the meadows with beautiful verdure, even so little acts of kindness cheer the family and brighten the world. Christ-like patience, coupled with paternal kindness and devoted filial affection, are the sweet blossoms of grace, which make the Home fragrant with a heart-refreshing and soul-inspiring atmosphere. May the reader resolve, by the grace of God, to help make his or her home a garden in which the beautiful and fragrant flowers of patience and kindness are constantly cultivated and grown to perfection.

Cheerfulness and **Contentment.**—This is another pair of twin graces, that should be carefully cultivated and given full sway in every home. Cheerfulness is a trait of character that brings sunshine and good cheer into the hearts and lives of all with whom it comes in contact. What the sun is to the earth with its various kinds of vegetation, what the stars are to the cloudless night, what God is to the burdened heart which knows how to lean upon Him, the cheerful person is to the Home, and the community. Cheerfulness is indeed sweet in infancy, lovely in youth, saintly in old age, and it ever carries with it refreshing influences all along the pathway of life.

Cheerfulness has the art of making all duty pleasant, all self-denial easy and desirable, all disappointments regarded as God's appointments, and it ever gives the dark clouds a silver lining.

The cheerful expressions of "Please," "Thank you," "Good morning," "How do you do?" "How are you faring?" "I wish you success," "What can I do for you?" etc., etc., if heartily and kindly spoken, help to make life brighter and more worthwhile, both within and outside of the Home.

Cheerfulness needs to be coupled with contentment, for neither can be perfected without the influence of the other. It is a blessed experience to be able to say with Paul, "I have learned, in whatsoever state I am, to be therewith content;" and especially so if contentment is coupled with godliness, because "godliness with contentment is great gain." Being in possession of this combination we can say with Paul, "Having food and raiment, let us be therewith content." Contentment is not founded upon the things that man possesses in the way of this world's wealth, position, and honor, but upon what man really is.

Great are the blessings which are enjoyed in the family, and they go forth from the Home as a sweet aroma to cheer and bless others, where the grace of cheerfulness and contentment are inculcated into the lives of its occupants.

Helpful Literature.—Every family should be amply supplied with good books, and other literature of a high moral and religious standard. At the head of the list should be the Book of all books, the Bible, which is the fountain source of everything that is elevating to the mind, comforting to the heart, inspiring to the soul, and refreshing to the spiritual life of man. It is the Book that records the incarnation of divine love; hence the best gift to men.

Books and periodicals are the most effective character-moulders in all the universe, either for good or evil. The voice that utters certain thoughts, or delivers the message may soon change or become silent forever. The heart that prompted the cheering message may grow cold and lifeless. But the books which convey to the reader those helpful thoughts and messages remain unchanged, and continue to wield a lasting influence upon those who read their immortal messages.

All books, periodicals, and other literature that may be of a questionable nature, should be eliminated from the Home. Good books are invaluable as a moral and religious guide to both young and old, and prove a safeguard against a multitude of evils. They are faithful companions and entertaining teachers that may be approached and consulted at any time, and always impart the same refreshing thoughts, wholesome advice, soul-inspiring counsel, and life-preserving principles.

Parents should not fail to supply their children with good, wholesome reading matter suitable to the age of each reader, and encourage them to form the habit of reading, which will have a tendency to keep them more closely connected with the Home and its helpful influences. When children have formed the habit of reading good books and periodicals, it creates in them a hunger and thirst for the things that are pure, and true, and noble, rather than to follow after vain and debasing pleasures of the world.

It is far better to deprive your children of pies, cakes, and other luxuries than to deprive them of literature that is needful to build up character. Great care should be exercised in selecting books and periodicals for reading and instruction, because the same has a lasting influence upon the mind, heart, and life of the reader. We often say, "A man is known by the company he keeps." It is equally true that a man's character may be, to a great extent, ascertained by the nature of the books he reads. Hence it is vitally essential for the safeguarding of the rising generation, that the family Library and reading table be kept free from everything along the literature line that is of a trashy or questionable nature.

To read with profit, the books must be of a kind that will give helpful information to the mind, and have a purifying effect upon the heart. To accomplish the most desirable results in the life of the individual, the Bible needs to be read and appreciated above all other books.

Daily family devotions and Bible study are the means of crowning the Home with the choicest of Heaven's blessings, because with the key of devoted prayer the store-house of God's divine treasures is unlocked and the same are showered upon the devoted suppliant. **Thomas Brooks,** has said: "The best and sweetest flowers in paradise, God gives to His people when they are on their knees in the closet. Prayer, if not the very gate of heaven, is the key to let us into its holiness and joys." True Christian devotion is the inseparable link that binds one to the triune God in the most sacred bonds of soul-satisfying communion.

The Bible needs to be more highly prized than any other book in the Home. Some of its sacred, soul-inspiring messages should be eagerly read each day in order to acquire the needed strength to perform life's duties both inside and outside the home. Through prayerful study of its rich comforting messages the soul is inspired and revived, and the spirit of devotion is developed and kept well balanced.

Those who daily listen to the voice of God through His precious Word can say with **Sir Wm. Jones:** "The Bible is the light of my understanding, the joy of my heart, the fullness of my hope, the clarifier of my affections, the mirror of my thoughts, the consoler of my sorrows, the guide of my soul through this gloomy labyrinth of time, the telescope sent from heaven to reveal to the eye of man the amazing glory of the far distant world.

"The Bible contains more true sublimity, more exquisite beauty, more pure morality, more important history, and finer strains of poetry and eloquence, than can be collected from all other books, in whatever age or language they may have been written."

An ideal family relationship exists in the home where every member of the family circle that has come to the years of accountability is a faithful, devoted Christian and identified with the divine institution called the Church. Thus the family ties become in the truest sense ideal, because the children are bound to the parental head by the ties of love and nature, and the entire family is bound to Christ the Head of the Church by divine love and devotion, as **R. F. Sample** has said: "Christ alone is the Head of the Church—by His truth to instruct it, by His authority to govern it, by His grace to quicken it, by His providence to protect and guide it, by His Holy Spirit to sanctify and bless it—the source of its life, wisdom, unity, peace, power, and prosperity; dwelling with it here on earth, and preparing its faithful members to dwell forever with Him in heaven."

In order to make every Christian Home as nearly ideal as possible, it is necessary for all who have been called to such a sacred charge, to look to the great fountain source of divine wisdom, grace and strength, and thus be enabled to make their immediate home a place where peace and harmony prevail, and where patience and forbearance have their perfect work; where sacrifices are made in loving service one toward another, the principles of honesty and truthfulness are taught by the parents, and practiced by every member of the family; where moral and religious instructions are thoughtfully, prayerfully, and diligently given; where children, young people, and parents, daily come to the throne of grace, to draw from God's inexhaustible treasury the necessary wisdom, grace, and strength to manfully fight life's battles; and where most of life's difficult problems are satisfactorily solved.

It is the sacred mission of every Christian Home to have within its walls the purest affections, the most desirable associations, the unquestioned evidences of fidelity; an atmosphere of quietude, peace, and harmony; an ever increasing spirit of true piety and devotion; a nursery in which the children are nourished and trained along lines of usefulness; a training school in which the most successful methods are used in teaching, directing, and training youthful lives to become useful in the master's service, and firmly stand for all that is noble, pure and good, that they may be a blessing to the world, a credit to society, a valuable asset to the Church, and an honor to God in helping to build up His cause on earth, by living devoted, loyal consecrated Christian lives. Such a Home is indeed an earthly Paradise, a beautiful type of the Blessed Home which the loving Father has prepared for His redeemed children in the Kingdom beyond.

BEAUTIFYING GEMS

Love is the choicest of Christian graces, a gem of inestimable value, the most fragrant of Eden's blossoms, the bond of domestic perfection, the most valuable parental gift, the most soothing balm for the troubled soul, the illuminating sun in the Christian home, and the rarest jewel among all earth's treasures.

*

True parental and filial love, coupled with divine love, is "the bond of perfectness," the cure for all domestic cares, sorrows, and wrongs, the golden link that binds us to truth and duty regardless of our weaknesses and imperfections. The power to love truly and devotedly is a gift of inestimable value.

*

Joy is the most soothing balm to ease and lighten the cares and disappointments in life, providing it has been divinely kindled through faith in Him who doeth all things well.

*

True domestic joys are worth infinitely more to the family than the finest artistic embellishments that can be used to decorate the Home.

*

"Whom having not seen, ye love; in whom, though now ye see him not, yet believing, ye rejoice with joy unspeakable and full of glory."—**Peter.**

*

Peace is a precious jewel, more precious than rubies. It does not dwell in the haunts of sin and vice, nor in domiciles of strife, but in the purified heart and consecrated soul, in homes where Christ has been enthroned as Head.

*

"Thou wilt keep him in perfect peace, whose mind is stayed on thee, because he trusteth in thee."—**Isaiah.**

*

"Honesty is the best policy." This is an old maxim, but those who are honest in their words, deeds, and business transactions, simply because it is good policy, are not truly honest. True honesty is founded upon the principles of righteousness, backed up by the Golden Rule.

The Home cannot be made ideal without honesty and domestic fidelity. True honesty takes into account the claims of both God and man, including those who are members of the family group. Honesty renders to God the things that are God's, and to man the things that are man's.

*

"Accustom your children to a strict attention to truth, even in the most minute particulars. If a thing happened at one window, and they, when relating it, say that it happened at the other, do not let it pass, but strictly check them; you do not know where deviations from truth will end."—**Johnson.**

*

"Economy is the parent of integrity, of liberty, and of ease; and the beauteous sister of temperance, of cheerfulness, and health; and profuseness is a cruel and crafty demon, that gradually involves her followers in dependence and debts, and so fetters them with irons that enter into their inmost souls."—**Hawkesworth.**

*

Relative to industry, it has been said, "If you have great talents, industry will improve them; if moderate abilities, industry will supply their deficiencies." Blessings are bestowed upon well directed labor, and nothing really worth while is attained without it. An hour's useful labor will do more to produce cheerfulness, suppress morbid feelings, and retrieve one's financial affairs, than a month's moaning.

*

Every member of the family should learn to be patient in little things, and learn to bear the every-day trials and annoyances of life quietly and calmly; and then, when unforeseen trouble or calamity comes, the strength to patiently endure will not forsake one. A patient, humble temper is a treasure, the value of which cannot be overestimated.

*

We should scatter the seeds of courtesy and kindness about us, at all times and under all conditions. Some of those precious seeds will fall on good ground, and grow up into trees of beauty and benevolence in the lives of others, and all of them will bear fruit of true happiness in the bosom from whence they sprang.

Cheerfulness is to
ers. It gives beauty, v
with which it comes in
way an influence that i
of others. Wondrous i
ening the burdens of
and in converting darkn

Contentment is a
coupled with the divine
spirit of godliness. To
coupled with true Chr
man can enjoy in this
the blessings of the fut